THE EVERYDAY LEADER

70-DAY DEVOTIONAL
GUIDE FOR LEADERS OF ALL AGES

VENNER J. ALSTON

BOOKS BY VENNER J. ALSTON

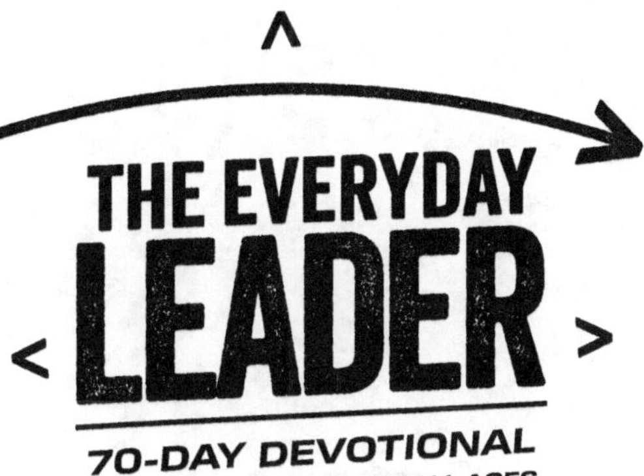

THE EVERYDAY LEADER

70-DAY DEVOTIONAL
GUIDE FOR LEADERS OF ALL AGES

VENNER J. ALSTON

VJAIM PUBLISHING

Published by VJ Alston International Ministries

1012 W Eldorado Pkwy, Suite 1175
Little Elm, TX 75068
drvjalston.org

Printed in the United States of America

ISBN 9798896199403

Unless otherwise noted, Scripture quotations in this publication are from The Passion Translation, copyright @2017, 2018 by Passion and Fire Ministries, Inc. Used by permission. All rights reserved.

Scripture quotation marked ESV are from the Easy-To-Read Version, copyright @2006 by the Bible League International.

Design Director Editorial Services: Rodriguez & Jones Translation Services

Cover & Interior Design by: David Quiroz Design

THE EVERYDAY LEADER

70-DAY DEVOTIONAL

GUIDE FOR LEADERS OF ALL AGES

VENNER J. ALSTON

INTRODUCTION

Welcome to The Everyday Leader: A 70-Day Devotional Guide for Leaders of All Ages. By offering daily inspiration and practical advice, this book helps you grow in your faith and leadership skills. You may be wondering, "Leadership? Me? I'm not a leader." If that's what you're wondering, think again. Every day, in even the simplest moments, opportunities for leadership arise. In the most ordinary things we do, we lead in ways we might not even realize. Whether we know it or not, we are constantly leading ourselves. This is our starting place, and it is what this book is all about.

Let's take a closer look at the nature of leadership. You may have thought of leadership as the power moves of someone higher up, someone in charge, one who inspires others or tells them what to do. But leadership is simpler than that. It is the ability to influence others toward a particular task or way of thinking, and we do it all the time. Think about your everyday conversations and the example you set in your actions. Whether you recognize it or not, you are an influencer. You may be a business owner, department manager, stay at home parent or student in pursuit of education, you are a leader. Now, consider how you interact with others. Is your influence positive? Are people happier, more hopeful, more productive, more loving when they've been around you? If they are, then there is something in you that calls it out in them. You need to identify and cultivate this capacity that helps others grow in faith and goodness. If you do, the more effective you will be.

Leadership is more than telling people what to do. It's a way of life, and it is both public and private. We lead by example. If we take a look around us, we can easily find examples of both good and bad leadership. You don't have to be on the glory road to be a leader. Unhealthy competitiveness, undermining others to get ahead, or justifying unethical tactics in the quest for recognition should not be the path the Christian leader takes. Authentic leadership is modeled through our lives and actions in the simplest, most ordinary things we do. But it doesn't happen without any effort. Your growth as a believer and leader requires daily nurturing. Join me on a journey as we explore biblical wisdom and learn how to follow Christian values and lead with integrity. It's time to deepen your faith in Christ and become the leader you were destined to be!

The daily readings, prayers, and reflections in this book follow the English alphabet. Each letter represents a foundational aspect of Christian leadership, providing you with a holistic and spiritually enriching approach to leadership development. My hope is that The Everyday Leader will empower you to lead each day with grace, compassion, and humility. At the same time, I encourage you to study the Gospels and draw inspiration from the teachings and leadership example of Jesus Christ, who at age thirty emerged as the most powerful leader in history. Understanding Jesus as a young, only thirty-year-old leader can be helpful for people of all ages. To young leaders, don't let your age keep you from embracing and developing your call to lead. For leaders in your middle or senior years of life, remember, you're not finished. It's not time to retire to the sidelines. The wisdom you have acquired can be invaluable to emerging young leaders as well as to more seasoned leaders who may be tempted to retreat from active roles. Lastly, to those of you who have never felt you were called to lead at all, stand straight and tall and come forth! The call to be an influencer was woven into your DNA before you were even born. It's not too late. You just have to recognize your leadership gifts. Start now!

Regardless of your age, consider the important qualities and principles of effective leadership that you can learn within the pages of this book. Set time aside for daily reading. Read the Gospels, too. As you look at Jesus' overflowing kindness and wisdom, and His ability to connect with all different kinds of people, you will see the value of being empathetic, inclusive, and dedicated to building strong, healthy relationships. Jesus' teachings about love, forgiveness, and helping others demonstrate the importance of authenticity. He was always direct and honest, and He calls us to be as truthful, tender, and self-giving as He was and still is!

There's something else He did, too, that we need to copy. The Gospels tell us that He made sure to spend lots of time with the Heavenly Father so that He could complete the difficult mandate upon His life. Let's examine His life. Look at His dedication to fulfilling the will of His Father in the face of great challenges. His example can motivate you to keep going and growing as both, a believer and leader. Following Jesus' leadership style of being humble, caring, and completely honest, and his focus on fairness, can inspire you to make a positive difference in your relationships, community, workplace, and beyond.

We are facing a rapidly changing world. In recent years, the changes have multiplied and accelerated, and we can't escape them. All the more reason to recognize and strengthen the power for good inside you as you find your way! So, I invite you to come along on this spiritual journey. Discover how to lead with purpose, courage, and love in all areas of your life, every day. Get ready to deepen your faith, strengthen your leadership skills, and become a powerful influencer who is equipped to navigate the unique challenges of your generation.

The memory scripture devotional, enhanced by journaling, serves as a transformative tool to cultivate a deeper connection with God, gain wisdom from His Word, and strengthen your leadership skills. Through the intentional practice of meditating on scripture and journaling, you can experience spiritual growth, personal reflection, and divine guidance in your journey of leadership and faith. Through consistent use, you will develop the prayer and study discipline necessary for your leadership development. Let this devotional guide be your spiritual companion and mentor as you seek to make a positive impact every day.

Each devotional is divided into five sections:

Memory Scripture Devotion:

Embrace each day with a heart eager to receive the scripture verse. Allow the Word to speak deeply to you, shaping your thoughts and actions throughout the day. Aspire to commit the daily verses to memory. Consider the insights of each devotional teaching, allowing the Holy Spirit to speak to you.

Personal Application:

Go deeper as you consider the verse's relevance to your life and leadership path. Allow its truths to affect your decisions and interactions, guiding you towards God's purpose for you.

Reflection:

Engage in thinking deeply, letting the scripture's profound message inspire your thoughts and stir your soul. Capture your reflections and revelations in your journal.

Affirmation:

Declare the scripture aloud with conviction and faith, affirming God's promises and power in your life. Let it be a beacon of hope and strength in your journey.

Prayer:

Conclude each devotional moment with heartfelt prayer, surrendering your desires and seeking God's guidance. Listen to His voice speaking within your soul. Trust in His faithfulness and provision as you step forward in leadership, knowing He is with you every step of the way, every day.

Journaling:

Some days may not include space for notes to allow room for deeper reflections. We encourage you to use your own journal and/ or the additional spaces provided to express your thoughts, prayers, insights, and aspirations as you walk alongside God in your leadership endeavors. Use this time and space to witness the transformation and growth in your spiritual journey, celebrate growth, and honor the work God is doing in your life through intentional expression.

Wherever you are in your leadership journey, as you apply the truths and insights you find in this devotional, you will experience daily growth. God has given each generation a unique call and purpose. You were created for great impact. To the young leader, you don't have to wait. You are needed! You are necessary to God's plan! Your time is now! To mature leaders, let your hard-won wisdom shine out. Each one of you is necessary! Let's go!

AMBITIONS ASPIRATIONS

> Before you do anything, put your trust totally in God and not in yourself. Then every plan you make will succeed.
> Proverbs 16:3 (TPT)

MEMORY SCRIPTURE

DEVOTIONAL

It is important to have ambitious aspirations and dreams. However, it is equally important to commit those aspirations to the Lord and seek His guidance. Perhaps you know someone who employs unhealthy tactics to gain promotions or recognition. They are following their own will, not trusting God. Aggressive tactics that don't honor the Lord are not the path we should ever take to promotion. Having a life plan is good and necessary, but our plans must agree with God's plans and methods. Proverbs 16:3 reminds us that when we commit our plans to the Lord, He will establish our steps. Trust in God's wisdom and guidance as you pursue your ambitious goals and know that He will lead you on the right path.

PERSONAL APPLICATION

Each day you must commit your plans to the Lord.

Reflect on your ambitious aspirations and be reminded of the potential within you. Consider the aspirations that you have had in the past. Were you mindful of aligning your dreams with His guidance? Be ready to take the first steps toward turning your dreams into reality with the Lord's help. Be willing to surrender those plans that do not agree with God's word, the Bible. Remember where your potential comes from!

 REFLECTION

Reflect on how these aspirations align with Kingdom values and how you can pursue them with integrity.

- ✔ Are your ambitions aligned with God's will for your life?
- ✔ Are you seeking His guidance and wisdom in all of your plans and aspirations?
- ✔ Take a moment to write down your most ambitious aspirations.
- ✔ Break them down into actionable steps and commit them to the Lord.

 AFFIRMATION

I am worthy of the ambitious dreams God has given me. I trust His guidance in the journey ahead. With faith and hard work, I will turn my aspirations into reality. I resist any negative influences that will limit my dreams. I will trust God's help to help me live the dream He has given me. I am willing to lay aside any aspirations that don't agree with the Bible.

 PRAYER

Lord, grant me the courage to dream big and the determination to pursue my aspirations. Help me to recognize any selfish ambitions that are outside of your plans for me. Give me your strength to lay aside every ambition that does not bring you glory and honor. Help me to follow the example of Jesus in pursuing my aspirations. Guide me so that I may walk on the path of ambition with humility and gratitude. Amen.

NOTES

ABIDING IN CHRIST

> *I am the sprouting vine and you're my branches. As you live in union with me as your source, fruitfulness will stream from within you - but when you live separated from me you are powerless.*
> John 15:5 (TPT)

MEMORY SCRIPTURE

 DEVOTIONAL

It is vital to stay connected to the source of true power and strength, which is Jesus Christ. Many leaders allow the busyness of life and leadership to move them away from their abiding place. To abide means to remain. When we abide, we are reliant upon Jesus as our Source of life and ministry. As a leader, you must recognize the importance of abiding in Christ, for apart from Him, you can do nothing. Just as a branch cannot bear fruit by itself unless it abides in the vine, choose to remain connected to Jesus, drawing strength, wisdom, and direction from Him in all that you do. Depending solely on yourself and your capabilities is the opposite of abiding in Christ.

 PERSONAL APPLICATION

Take a moment today to reflect on your relationship with Him.

Are you abiding in Him, seeking His guidance and wisdom in your decisions? Consider how you can deepen your connection with Jesus as your ultimate source of inspiration and strength. How can you deepen your connection with Christ in your daily life? In what areas of your leadership do you see the fruit of abiding in Christ evident, and where do you need to seek His guidance more intentionally?

REFLECTION

Reflect on the imagery of Jesus as the vine and us as the branches.

- ✔ Just as branches draw their life and nourishment from the vine, we derive our strength and vitality from our relationship with Christ. How can you incorporate the principle of abiding in Christ into your decision-making processes and interactions with others?

- ✔ Consider the areas in your life where you may have been trying to lead in your own strength, apart from Him.

- ✔ Acknowledge that true fruitfulness and success come from abiding in Him.

- ✔ Through abiding in Christ, trust that He will empower you to bear fruit, lead with love, and make a lasting impact for His kingdom.

AFFIRMATION

I am a branch connected to the vine, Jesus Christ. I choose to live in union with Him as my ultimate source of strength and inspiration. I will not follow the pattern of self-reliance but will fully trust in God's way. I believe that as I abide in Him, fruitfulness will flow from within me, and I will lead with purpose and effectiveness. I acknowledge my need for His power in my leadership journey, and I commit to staying connected to Him as my source of life.

PRAYER

Dear Jesus, thank you for being the vine that sustains me and the source of all strength and fruitfulness. Help me to abide in You daily, seeking Your wisdom and guidance. May Your power flow through me, enabling me to lead with grace, wisdom, and love. I resist anything designed to create barrenness and self-reliance in my life. Keep me connected to You, so that I may bear much fruit for Your glory. Amen.

NOTES

ACCOUNTABILITY IN COMMUNITY

> *My beloved friends, if you see a believer who is overtaken with a fault, the one who is in the Spirit should seek to restore him in the Spirit of gentleness. But keep watch over your own heart so that you won't be tempted to exalt yourself over him. Galatians 6:1-2 (TPT)*

MEMORY SCRIPTURE

 DEVOTIONAL

Embracing accountability in a community inspires you to walk in love and restoration towards others, fostering a culture of support and growth. It takes courage to confront a brother or a sister straying from the path of truth. Even so, do not turn a blind eye. Instead, lovingly, and gently guide them back, knowing that in doing so, you are saving precious lives and preventing further drift from God. Remember, our first leadership begins with leading ourselves. We can only hold others accountable in an honest and loving way if we're doing our best to face our own temptations and weaknesses. Accountability requires submission to God's word. It means caring enough for those whom God has placed around us to want them to have the joy and healing of a deeper relationship with God. By supporting and encouraging one another through accountability, you strengthen connections that foster growth and fulfill the law of Christ.

 PERSONAL APPLICATION

Endeavor to be a beacon of light and love in your community, always ready to extend a helping hand and lead others back to the Truth.

Leaders must be bold in embracing accountability within their community. Even when you make a mistake, you must be willing to forgive yourself as you receive God's forgiveness. Through accountability in community, you can carry each other's burdens, empowering yourself and others to grow and thrive in your leadership journey.

REFLECTION

Reflect on the importance of accountability in community, as outlined in Galatians 6:1-2.

- ✔ Consider a time when someone held you accountable in love. How did you respond?
- ✔ Consider the impact of restoring one another with gentleness and compassion and seeking to uplift and support those who have stumbled.
- ✔ Think about how accountability within a community of believers can lead to spiritual growth, unity, and a deeper understanding of the love of Christ.

AFFIRMATION

I affirm my commitment to fostering accountability within my community. I choose to approach moments of fault or struggle with gentleness and love, seeking restoration and growth for myself and those around me. I believe that accountability within a supportive community empowers us to fulfill the law of Christ and carry each other's burdens with grace and compassion.

PRAYER

Dear God, thank you for the gift of community and accountability. Help me to embrace accountability with a spirit of love and restoration, seeking to uplift and support others in their times of need. Help me to respond in a spirit of love and humility when I myself am being held accountable in an area of my life. Grant me the wisdom and courage to hold myself and others accountable in a way that reflects Your grace and compassion. May our community be a place of growth, unity, and mutual support as we walk in accountability together. Amen.

NOTES

____

____

____

Boldly Break Barriers

> *For God will never give you the spirit of fear, but the Holy Spirit who gives you mighty power, love, and self-control. 2 Timothy 1:7 (TPT)*

MEMORY SCRIPTURE

 ## DEVOTIONAL

Breaking through barriers requires courage. Barriers can be either self-imposed or imposed upon us by others or by circumstances beyond our control. These barriers have not passed through the lens of God's love. When this happens, we become fearful that we cannot do what God has created us for. We can even feel stopped or trapped. But the scripture reminds us that even if we feel afraid, fear is not from God. Fear can stop our growth and development. With His Spirit within you, in spite of those feelings of fear, you can face obstacles boldly and grow through challenging times. Gratefully acknowledge the lessons you've learned in overcoming barriers and keep growing in confidence. After all, as Romans 8:31 says, "If God is for us, who can be against us?"

 ## PERSONAL APPLICATION

Remember that you are equipped with a spirit of power, love, and self-discipline by the Holy Spirit who dwells within you.

Fear creates barriers and limitations. Let go of fear and embrace the confidence that comes from knowing you are called and empowered to make a difference. Often, when we compare ourselves to others, we overlook wonderful areas of our own life. This creates a barrier within us. Step boldly into your leadership role, trusting in God's strength within you to overcome any obstacles designed to limit you and hinder your progress and growth.

 REFLECTION

Identify one barrier that has been holding you back.

- ✔ What were your emotions telling you during this challenging time?
- ✔ What does the Bible say about this challenge?
- ✔ Take time to create a plan to overcome it, embracing the power and love that God has instilled in you.
- ✔ Take a bold step forward, trusting in His guidance.
- ✔ As you reflect on the experience, realize the strength you possess through the indwelling Holy Spirit.

AFFIRMATION

I am a barrier-breaker. I resist every assignment of fear designed to create barriers or limitations in my life and leadership. I will not fear! Fear has no power over me. Therefore, I embrace challenges as opportunities to grow stronger. The Holy Spirit is my Helper!

PRAYER

Heavenly Father, empower me to break through the barriers that limit my potential. As I present my challenges to you, I refuse every thought that creates fear. Strengthen my resolve to face challenges with boldness and resilience. Help me to see your power working within me and for me every day. Help me daily to boldly, gratefully, and courageously express your power. Amen.

NOTES

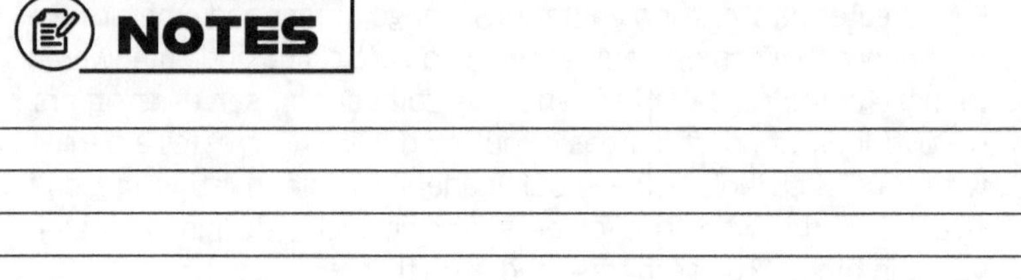

BUILDING AUTHENTIC RELATIONSHIPS

> *People learn from each other, as one iron tool can make another one sharp.*
> Proverbs 27:17 (Easy)

MEMORY SCRIPTURE

 DEVOTIONAL

It is crucial to surround yourself with mentors and peers who will challenge you, inspire you, and help you become the best leader you can be. Just as iron sharpens iron, your relationships can sharpen your character and leadership skills. Some apparent leaders rely only on their own capacity. They overlook the power of strong life-giving relationships, which create authenticity, transparency, accountability, and growth. Take some time today to reflect on the people in your life who have influenced you positively in your leadership journey. How have they helped you grow and become a better leader?

 PERSONAL APPLICATION

Evaluate the authenticity of your relationships. Building authentic relationships with others can help you grow, learn, and become an effective leader.

How can you sharpen and be sharpened by those around you? Think about the relationships you have with other leaders. Are there any who are helping you grow and develop as a leader? Are there any who are hindering your progress or holding you back? Authentic relationships can be a source of strength, encouragement, and support as you navigate the challenges of leadership.

 REFLECTION

Consider the impact of meaningful relationships on your spiritual journey.

- ✔ How have you isolated yourself and resisted transparency?
- ✔ In what relationships have you been willing to be transparent?
- ✔ Have you allowed yourself to be sharpened in certain moments?
- ✔ How have your relationships shaped your character?
- ✔ Consider how you can cultivate positive, supportive relationships which will encourage and challenge you to reach your full potential.
- ✔ How can you be not only a better leader but also a better friend?

 AFFIRMATION

I am a leader who is constantly growing and learning. I am grateful for the mentors and peers who sharpen my character and leadership skills. I will seek out relationships that inspire me, challenge me, and support me on my journey to becoming a strong and effective leader. I will be a good friend to others, listening, supporting, and being honest with them.

 PRAYER

Dear God, thank you for placing mentors and peers in my life who sharpen my character and leadership skills. Help me to be a positive influence on other potential leaders and to seek out relationships that will push me to grow and excel in my leadership role. Guide me in fostering healthy, uplifting connections with others who will inspire and support me on my leadership journey. Amen.

NOTES

BOLDNESS IN FAITH

> *So now we draw near freely and boldly to where grace is enthroned, to receive mercy's kiss and discover the grace we urgently need to strengthen us in our time of weakness.*
> *Hebrews 4:16 (TPT)*

MEMORY SCRIPTURE

 DEVOTIONAL

As a leader, it is important to remember that you can boldly approach God's throne of grace at any time. This means that you can come to Him with confidence, knowing that He is ready to extend His mercy and grace to you. During challenging times some leaders retreat into themselves and feel overwhelmed by the demands of the day. Consequently, the courage to stand boldly eludes them. At such times, we must accept that our human capacity is limited and therefore draw our strength from God and not from ourselves.

 PERSONAL APPLICATION

Take a moment today to reflect on how you can incorporate this truth into your leadership.

How can you rely on God's grace and seek His help when you are faced with challenges or decisions? What issues are confronting you where you are lacking the courage to boldly present your needs and fears to the Lord? Remember that His throne of grace is always open to you, offering help when you need it most.

 REFLECTION

Think about the times when you have needed God's grace and mercy.

- ✔ Even if you felt afraid, were you able to reach out to Him and seek His help anyway?
- ✔ When you did, how did He provide for you and help you overcome obstacles?
- ✔ Reflect on the ways in which God's grace has sustained you and empowered you to lead with confidence and compassion.

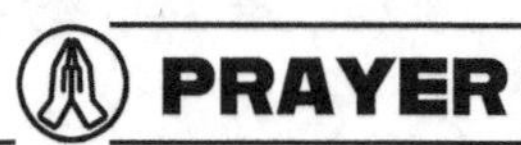 AFFIRMATION

I choose to boldly approach God's throne of grace, knowing that He will extend His mercy and grace to me in times of need. I trust that His grace will equip me to lead with wisdom and humility, and His mercy will guide me through challenges and uncertainties. I am confident in His provision and support as I navigate my leadership responsibilities.

PRAYER

Dear God, thank you for inviting me to boldly approach Your throne of grace. I come to You with confidence, seeking Your mercy and grace to help me to be a positive influencer. Grant me wisdom and discernment as I make decisions and fill me with Your strength and compassion to lead others effectively. May Your grace sustain me, and Your mercy guide me as I lead with humility and love. Amen.

NOTES

COLLABORATE AND CONQUER

> **"** *Two people who work together are better than one person who works alone. They can help each other to work well. If one of them falls down, his friend can help him to get up, But it is terrible if you fall down when you are alone. Ecclesiastes 4:9,10 (Easy)* **"**

MEMORY SCRIPTURE

 DEVOTIONAL

As a Christian leader, embracing the principle of collaboration is key to conquering challenges and achieving success. Reflect on the importance of working together with others who share your vision and values. Consider how you can foster partnerships and alliances that will strengthen and support you as you strive to make a positive impact in your leadership role. We can best accomplish our goals when we welcome each other's insights and strengths. Reliance on our capabilities alone, limits both our resources and our outcomes. Choose today to see the possibilities of powerful collaborations around you.

 PERSONAL APPLICATION

Today, reach out to a colleague or friend for a collaborative effort.

Remember to actively listen to their ideas, share your own, and appreciate the collective strength that comes from working together. Think about the power of teamwork and collaboration in your leadership endeavors. Did the collaborative effort not only bring success but also deepen your understanding of the power of teamwork?

🔍 REFLECTION

Consider how partnering with like-minded individuals can help you overcome obstacles, leverage strengths, and reach your goals more effectively.

- ✔ Did the scripture's wisdom about the synergy of two different people resonate with your experience?
- ✔ Was the outcome greater than you could have accomplished alone?
- ✔ Were you inspired to continue embracing collaboration in all aspects of your life?
- ✔ Remember that together you can conquer any challenge that comes your way.

💬 AFFIRMATION

I affirm that collaboration is essential for achieving success and making a difference in the world. I acknowledge the value of working with others who can offer support, guidance, and encouragement to me. I choose to embrace the principle of collaboration and conquer challenges collectively with a spirit of unity and teamwork. I resist any tendencies to isolate myself from others, especially during challenging times.

🙏 PRAYER

Dear God, thank you for the gift of collaboration and partnerships. Help me to recognize the importance of working together with others to achieve common goals and fulfill Your purpose for all our lives. Grant me the wisdom to build strong alliances and foster relationships that will empower and uplift me as I lead. May my collaborative efforts be guided by Your wisdom and grace, enabling me to conquer challenges and make a positive impact in the world. Amen.

📝 NOTES

COMPASSION FOR OTHERS

> *God has chosen you to be his own special people. You belong to him and he loves you very much. So this is how you should live: Be kind to other people and help them. Do not think that you are better than other people. Instead, respect them and be patient with them. Colossians 3:12 (Easy)*

MEMORY SCRIPTURE

 DEVOTIONAL

As you lead, it is important to reflect the character of God in your leadership style. This verse reminds us of the importance of showing compassion towards others. As leaders, it is essential to treat those around us with kindness, humility, and patience. By demonstrating compassion, we reflect the love of God and create a positive impact on those we lead. Take some time today to consider how you can embody qualities such as mercy, kindness, humility, gentleness, and patience in your interactions with others.

 PERSONAL APPLICATION

Has there been a time when you needed the compassion of others?

Too often, we look at the circumstances of others without compassion. We form a judgment that their circumstance is somehow their own fault. Recall a time when you yourself needed someone to show compassion to you, and it was not shown. How did you feel at that moment? Now, use your own experience of judgment and rejection to show compassion to someone in need. How can you embody Christ's love in practical ways? How can these virtues enhance your leadership effectiveness and influence those around you positively? Consider how you might better listen and show compassion to others.

REFLECTION

Jesus' acts of judging, aimed at bringing about repentance, transformation, and reconciliation with God, were rooted in love, truth, and righteousness.

- ✔ Reflect on the ways in which God's love and grace have shaped your identity.

- ✔ Judging occurs when we unfairly criticize or condemn others without acknowledging our own mistakes. How do you see Jesus demonstrating righteous judgement with kindness and compassion instead?

- ✔ Consider the impact that demonstrating mercy, kindness, humility, gentleness, and patience can have on fostering a positive and inclusive environment within your leadership sphere. How can you integrate compassion toward others in your leadership?

- ✔ Think about specific situations where these qualities can make a difference and lead by example.

AFFIRMATION

I affirm that I am chosen and loved by God. I choose to clothe myself with mercy, kindness, humility, gentleness, and patience in all aspects of my life. These qualities reflect the character of God and empower me to lead with compassion and wisdom. I embrace the responsibility to make a positive impact on those around me and strive to be a shining example of God's love and grace in my leadership journey.

PRAYER

Lord, help me to always walk in mercy, kindness, humility, gentleness, and patience as I lead others. Grant me the wisdom and strength to embody Your character in all that I do and may Your love shine through me as I serve in my leadership role. Guide me in showing grace and compassion to those around me, and may my leadership reflect Your boundless love. Amen.

COURAGE IN UNCERTAINTY

> *Remember, that I have told you this: Be strong and do not be afraid. Do not be weak but be brave, I the Lord your God will be with you everywhere that you go.*
> *Joshua 1:9 (Easy)*

MEMORY SCRIPTURE

DEVOTIONAL

Leadership is bound to take us into places of uncertainty. We often don't know how we ever got there. All we know is that we're suddenly faced with tough, unexpected decisions. In the midst of uncertainty, Joshua 1:9 calls us to be strong and courageous, confident that God is ever present by our side. When the path ahead is unclear, we can't help feeling unprepared and unsure about what to do. The fear of making decisions can be overwhelming. At those moments, it is important to remember God is with us, and God is always prepared, especially when we are not. Remember that Jesus constantly walked a road where He never really knew whom He would meet or what He would have to do. But He walked it anyway. Like Jesus, let God's promise of unwavering support and guidance instill in you the courage needed to walk the uncertain road of leadership. Embrace the unknown with faith and boldness, trusting in God's constant presence to lead you and be with you.

 PERSONAL APPLICATION

How do you respond during times of uncertainty?

Under which circumstances have you lacked courage? What causes you to feel uncertain and unsettled? Reflect on these moments where courage is needed. Consider the unknowns, the challenges, and the risks that lie ahead. How can you draw strength from God's promise to be with you and cultivate courage to navigate the uncertainties with faith and confidence?

 REFLECTION

Reflect on the significance of courage in times of uncertainty, as highlighted in Joshua 1:9.

- ✔ Think about moments when fear and doubt have clouded your path. How has God's presence and assurance of being with you given you the courage needed to press forward and lead with conviction?
- ✔ Reflect on the ways in which you can embrace courage as a beacon of hope in the midst of uncertainty.
- ✔ Decide to submit these areas of uncertainty to the Lord.

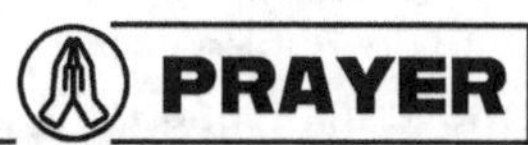 AFFIRMATION

I affirm my commitment to embodying courage in the face of uncertainty. I choose to trust in God's presence, purpose, and promise, knowing that He goes before me and is my strength. I believe that with His guidance, I can overcome fear and lead with boldness, resilience, and unwavering faith in the midst of unknown circumstances.

 PRAYER

Dear Lord, grant me the courage to face uncertainty in my leadership journey. Help me to be strong and brave, trusting in Your unfailing presence and guidance. May Your assurance of being with me wherever I go, fill me with the courage needed to navigate challenges and make decisions with confidence. Lead me forward in faith, knowing that Your strength sustains me in times of uncertainty. Amen.

NOTES

COMPASSIONATE HEART

> *Lay aside bitter words, temper tantrums, revenge, profanity, and insults. But instead, be kind and affectionate toward one another. Has God graciously forgiven you? Then graciously forgive one another in the depths of Christ's love. Eph. 4:31,32 (TPT)*

 DEVOTIONAL

In Ephesians 4:31-32, we are called to embody a spirit of compassion through forgiveness. Too many people allow bitterness and anger to become their constant companion. They think anger and bitterness are signs of strength and never realize how false and empty their chosen companions are. Forgiveness is real strength, and there is nothing empty about it. The ability to extend forgiveness to others is the endless power of compassion and grace, just as Jesus extended it to us. Life is full of undeserved suffering, and it can be hard to let go of bitterness and anger. Follow the example of Jesus! He did not deserve the Cross, but His last words were about forgiveness. Be like Him and offer kindness and understanding no matter where you find yourself. Just as God has graciously forgiven us, we are urged to extend that same grace and forgiveness to those around us.

 PERSONAL APPLICATION

Embrace forgiveness today as a form of compassion and choose to release any feelings of resentment or hurt.

Offer forgiveness and understanding to those who may have caused you pain. Try to walk in their shoes and remember your own mistakes. Are you struggling to forgive yourself for mistakes you've made? Forgiveness is not only for others but also for ourselves. God works with us to help us let go of hurtful things we have done so that we can start a new chapter of life. When we don't forgive ourselves or others, we remain fixed in that moment of time, rehearsing the event over and over rather than seeking the healing of forgiveness.

Forgiveness means a new chance at life where compassion reigns, both toward us and to others. Seek to cultivate a heart of compassion through the act of forgiveness, recognizing the healing and unity it can bring to relationships and within your own life. Forgiveness opens the boundaries of life. By extending grace and forgiveness, create a culture of compassion and empathy not only toward yourself but far beyond. Then watch for new horizons!

 REFLECTION

Take a moment to reflect on the concept of forgiveness as a powerful form of compassion in your leadership approach.

- ✔ Consider the impact that extending forgiveness can have on fostering healing, reconciliation, undreamed possibilities, and unity.

- ✔ Reflect on the transformative nature of forgiveness and how it can lead to stronger relationships.

- ✔ What hurts have you sustained that you feel that you cannot forgive?

- ✔ How can you set yourself free through God's word and promises?

- ✔ How can you practice forgiveness as a profound expression of compassion towards others in your leadership role?

AFFIRMATION

I choose to let go of bitterness and anger, and instead, I extend forgiveness and grace to those around me. I choose to forgive myself for past sins and errors I have made. Through the transformative power of forgiveness, I create a culture of healing, reconciliation, and unity. I believe that by showing compassion through forgiveness, I can build a community of empathy, understanding, and grace in my leadership journey.

 PRAYER

Dear God, grant me the courage and strength to practice forgiveness as a form of compassion towards myself and others. Help me release any grudges or hurt, and instead, extend grace and forgiveness to those who may have wronged me. Guide me in showing compassion and understanding through the act of forgiveness, fostering healing and unity with family, friends, and co-workers. May forgiveness be a testament to your love and compassion in all that I do. Amen.

NOTES

ADDITIONAL NOTES

ADDITIONAL NOTES

DISCERNMENT IN DECISION-MAKING

Trust in the Lord completely, and do not rely on your own opinions. With all your heart rely on Him to guide you, and He will lead you in every decision you make. Become intimate with Him in whatever you do, and He will lead you wherever you go. Proverbs 3:5-6 (TPT)

MEMORY SCRIPTURE

 DEVOTIONAL

As leaders, we are faced with countless decisions each day that shape our paths and impact those around us. Far too often we make decisions without seeking God's will. In other words, we don't have all of the facts. We tend to make decisions in haste based on our own opinions. In the midst of uncertainty and pressure, it is crucial to rely on the wisdom and guidance of the Lord in our decision-making process. Trusting in Him completely and seeking His direction with all our hearts will lead us on the right path and bring clarity in our choices.

 PERSONAL APPLICATION

Today, commit to trusting in the Lord completely and seeking His guidance in all your decisions.

Do not rely on your own understanding or opinions, but instead, seek to become intimate with Him in every aspect of your life. Spend time seeking the council of the Lord. Invite His wisdom to lead you in every choice you make, knowing that His direction is always best. God gives us signs in the most surprising places. Pay attention. Listen for His voice speaking in the world around you. Listen for His voice speaking in your heart.

REFLECTION

Take a moment to reflect on a recent decision you made.

✔ Did you seek God's guidance in the process?

✔ How do you think the outcome would have been different if you had relied on Him completely?

✔ Do you have others who can provide counsel and help you to pray during times of decision making?

✔ How can you incorporate more trust and intimacy with God in your decision-making moving forward?

AFFIRMATION

I am a leader who trusts in the Lord completely. I rely on His wisdom and guidance in every decision I make, knowing that He will lead me on the right path. I will seek the counsel of God and other mature leaders in my decision making. I am intimate with Him in all that I do, allowing His direction to shape my choices and bring clarity to my journey. I will pay attention and listen for His voice.

PRAYER

Father, I come before you today seeking your wisdom and guidance in my decision-making. Help me to trust in you completely and not lean on my own understanding. Thank you for connecting me with other mature leaders and for leading me in every choice I make. Help me to become intimate with you in all aspects of my life. May your direction bring clarity and purpose to my path. Amen.

NOTES

DARE TO DREAM DIFFERENTLY

> *Stop imitating the ideals and opinions of the culture around you but be inwardly transformed by the Holy Spirit through a total reformation of how you think. This will empower you to discern God's will as you live a beautiful life, satisfying and perfect in his eyes. Romans 12:2 (TPT)*

MEMORY SCRIPTURE

DEVOTIONAL

Renew your mind and transform your leadership approach by embracing Romans 12:2's call not to be conformed to this world but transformed by the renewing of your mind. Don't fall into the trap of worldliness by choosing to follow the example of unbelievers rather than to follow the example of Jesus. How are you letting your old mindsets and behaviors still be part of you? Allow the Holy Spirit to shape your perspective and leadership style, guiding you to lead with wisdom, discernment, and compassion. Surrender to His transformative work within you and watch as your leadership positively impacts those around you.

PERSONAL APPLICATION

Today, spend time in quiet reflection, allowing your mind to break free from conventional thinking.

How is your old life prohibiting you from dreaming God's dream for your life? How are you choosing to walk in the path of the unregenerate version of you so that you cannot see the innovation God wants to bring to you? What are your deepest dreams, the ones you would dare to follow if you weren't listening to the world? Write down at least three dreams, even if they seem to be completely out of reach and contemplate the first steps toward bringing them to life. Challenge yourself to change your dreams from impossible to possible by seeking God's guidance and wisdom in your aspirations. Allow the Holy Spirit to transform your thinking and align your dreams with His will. Although change feels scary, allow Him to change you. Embrace the beauty of living a life that is pleasing to God and strive to make choices that reflect His values and purposes for you as a leader.

🔍 REFLECTION

As you reflect on the dreams and aspirations you have for your life; do they align with God's will and purpose for you?

- ✔ How can you allow the Holy Spirit to renew your mind and guide you in daring to dream differently?

- ✔ Consider how stepping out in faith and trusting in God's plan can lead to a life that is truly satisfying and perfect in His eyes.

- ✔ Has the process of daring to dream differently opened your mind to new possibilities?

- ✔ The scripture instructs us of the transformative power of breaking free from societal norms. As you reflect, do you feel a sense of liberation and excitement about the potential impact of your unique God-given dreams?

💬 AFFIRMATION

I dare to dream differently, and my unique vision contributes to the positive transformation of myself and the world around me. I am a leader who dares to dream differently. I am not conformed to the patterns of this world, but I am transformed by the renewing of my mind through the Holy Spirit. I have the power to discern God's will and live a life that is beautiful, satisfying, and perfect in His eyes.

🙏 PRAYER

God, inspire me to see beyond the ordinary and unchanging and dream differently. Dear Lord, thank you for the gift of transformation through your Holy Spirit. Help me to break free from the influence of the world and dare to dream that things which seem impossible are possible with You. Guide me in discerning your will for my life and give me the courage to pursue a path that is aligned with your purposes. May my dreams be inspired by You and bring glory to your name. Amen.

📝 NOTES

____

____

____

____

____

____

DEPENDENCE ON GOD'S WORD

> *Truth's shining light guides me in my choices and decisions; the revelation of your word makes my pathway clear. Psalm 119:105 (TPT)*

MEMORY SCRIPTURE

 DEVOTIONAL

As a leader, you are constantly faced with important choices and decisions that shape your life and impact those around you. Perhaps, before you were a believer, you totally relied on yourself or the influences of the culture in which you lived. Perhaps you struggled to make decisions and felt paralyzed. As a follower of Christ, you don't have to struggle with uncertainty. Amid uncertainty and confusion, you can find clarity and direction by depending on the truth and guidance found in God's Word. His Word is a shining light that illuminates your path and leads you in the way you should go.

 PERSONAL APPLICATION

Consider the ways in which you can incorporate more dependence on God's Word into your daily life and decision-making process.

God's Word is full of signposts showing you the way. Make it your regular practice to look for them. Align your thoughts and actions with the teachings of God's Word, trusting that His guidance will lead you in the right direction.

 REFLECTION

Take a moment to reflect on a time when you sought guidance from God's Word in a decision you had to make.

- ✔ How did you experience clarity in those moments?
- ✔ Maybe you were moved to read a particular psalm or Bible story, though you did not know why. Perhaps when you were most perplexed, words of Scripture suddenly came to mind. How did God's truth and revelation impact your decision?
- ✔ How can you spend consistent time in prayer and meditation on Scripture, seeking the truth, and wisdom that will make your pathway clear?

 AFFIRMATION

: I am a leader who depends on God's Word for guidance. I will commit to depending on God's Word for guidance in my choices and decisions. When the way forward is cloudy and I cannot see my way, His truth shines light on my path and makes my decisions clear. I trust in His revelation to lead me in the way I should go, knowing that His Word is a source of wisdom and direction in all aspects of my life.

 PRAYER

Lord, thank you for the gift of your Word, which serves as a guiding light in my life. Help me to depend on your truth and revelation in all my choices and decisions. Illuminate my path with the wisdom found in Scripture and guide me in the way I should go. May my dependence on your Word lead me to make choices that honor and glorify you. Amen.

NOTES

DILIGENCE IN SERVICE

> " *Put your heart and soul into every activity you do, as though you are doing it for the Lord himself and not merely for others. For we know that we will receive a reward, an inheritance from the Lord, as we serve the Lord Yahweh, the Anointed One! Colossians 3:23-24 (TPT)* "

DEVOTIONAL

As you embark on your journey as a leader, remember Colossians 3:23-24's call to put your heart and soul into every task as unto the Lord. Leaders should be committed to fully executing tasks assigned to them. If you commit to a task, you should be faithful to your commitment and make time to do as you promised. Let diligence and excellence characterize your service, knowing that your efforts are ultimately an offering to God. Trust that, as you serve with passion and integrity, you will receive a reward and inheritance from the Lord, fueling your commitment to lead with purpose and devotion.

PERSONAL APPLICATION

As a leader, commit to approaching every task, responsibility, and interaction with diligence and wholeheartedness, knowing that your service is ultimately unto the Lord.

Resist following poor leadership examples that take the easy way out and do not honor God. Reflect on your current attitude towards your leadership role and responsibilities. How can you infuse your service with passion, excellence, and a heart that honors God in all you do?

REFLECTION

Reflect on the call to diligence in service as outlined in Colossians 3:23-24.

- ✔ Consider the impact of viewing your leadership responsibilities as acts of worship to the Lord, rather than mere obligations to others.
- ✔ Is yours a motive of service unto God or is it just to please people?
- ✔ How does the promise of a reward and inheritance from the Lord motivate you to serve with excellence, integrity, and a heart that seeks to honor Him in all things?

AFFIRMATION

I affirm my commitment to serve with diligence, excellence, and wholehearted devotion as a leader in everything I do. I choose to approach every task and interaction as an opportunity to honor God and serve Him with passion and integrity. I believe that as I put my heart and soul into His service, I honor Him and my efforts are seen and valued by Him.

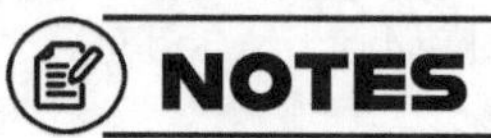

PRAYER

Lord, I thank You for the privilege of serving as a leader in Your kingdom. Help me to approach my responsibilities with diligence, excellence, and a heart that seeks to honor You in all I do. May my service be a reflection of my love and devotion to You, as I work wholeheartedly unto You and not merely for others. Grant me the strength, wisdom, and passion to lead with integrity and excellence, knowing that my reward comes from serving You, the Anointed One. Amen.

NOTES

EMPOWERED BY THE SPIRIT

> *But I promise you this—the Holy Spirit will come upon you, and you will be seized with power. You will be my messengers to Jerusalem, throughout Judea, the distant provinces—even to the remotest places on earth! Acts 1:8 (TPT)*

MEMORY SCRIPTURE

 ## DEVOTIONAL

Before you became a follower of Christ, you had not accessed His promise of supernatural power and strength in your life. As you have chosen to follow Him, the promise of empowerment by the Holy Spirit as declared in Acts 1:8 is now available to you. You no longer need to rely solely on your own strength. Allow the Holy Spirit's power to equip and guide you in your leadership journey, enabling you to be a bold messenger of God's love and truth to those around you. Embrace the Holy Spirit's empowering presence as a source of strength, wisdom, and courage as you step into your role as a leader every day.

 ## PERSONAL APPLICATION

Reflect on how you can actively seek the empowerment of the Holy Spirit in your leadership endeavors.

In what areas of your life are you depending on your own strength and not on His? Consider the areas in your life where you may need the Spirit's guidance and strength to fulfill your calling to lead and overcome challenging situations. Commit to inviting the Holy Spirit to work through you, empowering you to lead with boldness, compassion, and a heart set on fulfilling God's purposes.

 REFLECTION

Reflect on the significance of being filled with the power of the Holy Spirit, as emphasized in Acts 1:8.

- ✔ Consider the impact of relying on the Holy Spirit's guidance and strength in your leadership roles and responsibilities.
- ✔ How does the promise of being God's messenger to various spheres of influence inspire you to lead with purpose and passion, knowing that you are empowered by the Holy Spirit for such a time as this?
- ✔ What challenging situations do you need to submit to the Holy Spirit for guidance and strength?

AFFIRMATION

I affirm my belief in the empowering presence of the Holy Spirit in every area of my life. I choose to rely on the Spirit's guidance, strength, and power as I lead others with courage and conviction. I believe that as I embrace the Spirit's empowerment, I am equipped to be a messenger of God's love and truth, impacting lives and fulfilling His purposes in the world.

PRAYER

Lord, thank you for the promise of being filled with the power of the Holy Spirit as I lead and serve in Your kingdom. I pray for a fresh outpouring of Your Spirit upon me, equipping me to be a bold and effective leader. May the Spirit's guidance and strength empower me to fulfill Your calling in my life, and to be a messenger of Your love and truth to those I encounter. Grant me the wisdom and courage to lead with humility and grace, reflecting Your character in all I do. Amen.

 NOTES

____

____

____

ENCOURAGING OTHERS

> **"**
>
> *Because of this, encourage the hearts of your fellow believers and support one another, just as you have already been doing.*
> *1 Thessalonians 5:11 (TPT)*
>
> **"**

MEMORY SCRIPTURE

 ## DEVOTIONAL

Everyone needs encouragement at some point. Too many people spend time discouraging and mocking others whom they perceive to be different or less gifted and talented than themselves. You have the power to radiate hope and unity through your words and actions, as 1 Thessalonians 5:11 urges you to do. Embrace the opportunity to uplift those around you with encouraging words and gestures, fostering a sense of inclusivity and support within your community.

 ## PERSONAL APPLICATION

Let your leadership be a beacon of positivity and inspiration, ensuring that everyone feels valued and empowered to thrive.

How can you intentionally incorporate encouragement and hope into the lives of others? Consider ways in which you can brighten someone's day with a kind word or gesture, creating a culture of positivity and support. Be intentional about looking for the giftedness in others and celebrating their accomplishments. Commit to being a source of light and encouragement, spreading hope and unity wherever you go. With your warmth and caring, lift other people up!

 REFLECTION

Reflect on the transformative impact of speaking life-giving words and building hope within your sphere of influence, as outlined in 1 Thessalonians 5:11.

- ✔ Consider the ripple effect of your encouragement on those around you, uplifting spirits and igniting a sense of togetherness and solidarity.

- ✔ Identify someone who has been having a difficult time in their life or career. How can you encourage them?

- ✔ How can you continue to cultivate a community where everyone is valued and included, where they are motivated to pursue their dreams and aspirations?

AFFIRMATION

I affirm my dedication to being a beacon of hope and unity in my leadership journey, following the example set by 1 Thessalonians 5:11. Like Jesus, I choose to speak words of encouragement, build up hope, and foster inclusivity and support among those I lead. I believe that through my actions, I can inspire and empower others to embrace their unique gifts and talents, creating a harmonious and uplifting environment for growth and success.

PRAYER

Heavenly Father, thank You for entrusting me with the opportunity to spread hope and unity through my leadership. Grant me the strength and wisdom to be a source of encouragement to those around me, uplifting spirits and fostering a sense of togetherness. May my words and actions reflect Your love and grace, inspiring others to embrace their full potential and walk in unity and purpose. Help me to follow the example set by Jesus. Guide me in creating a culture of positivity and support, where everyone feels valued and included. Amen.

 NOTES

____

____

____

FEARLESSLY FORGE FUTURES

> " : I, the Lord, tell you this: I have decided what I will do for you. I have plans to help you to do well. I do not want to hurt you. I want to give you hope for a good life in the future.
> Jeremiah 29:11 (Easy) "

MEMORY SCRIPTURE

 DEVOTIONAL

Jeremiah 29:11 is a reminder of God's promise to provide you with a future filled with hope and purpose. Feelings that there is no possible bright future are all too common in our society. Fear of failure, not having enough education to get a decent job, a history of unsatisfactory relationships, a disability, or even a lack of models of success in our families can create a mindset of anger and despair. No matter how great the drawbacks are, do not give in to them! Trust that God has planned a future for you, and it is good! Embrace this assurance as you fearlessly forge ahead in your life, giving everything you are to it, and trusting that God's plans for you are filled with promise. Let this verse inspire you to lead with courage, vision, and a steadfast faith in God's guiding hand.

 PERSONAL APPLICATION

How you can apply the promise of Jeremiah 29:11 to your endeavors? If you lack models of success among your friends and family, dare to envision your ideal future anyway. Believe in it and claim it.

Consider areas in your life where fear may be hindering you from stepping boldly into the future that God has planned for you. Write down the steps you need to take to bring this vision to reality, acknowledging that God's plans for you are filled with hope and possibility. Look for people who may be doing the good work you are dreaming about and listen to their stories or read their books. Often you will find that they have overcome obstacles as great or even greater than yours. You can, too. Commit to embracing a fearless mindset, trusting in God's faithfulness and provision as you lead with confidence and purpose.

🔍 REFLECTION

Reflect on the profound truth that God has thoughts of peace and a future filled with hope for you, as declared in Jeremiah 29:11.

- ✔ Consider how this promise can shape your perspective on the challenges and opportunities that lie ahead in your leadership journey.

- ✔ As you reflect on forging your future, were you comforted by the scripture's assurance of God's plans for your well-being?

- ✔ You were not created for failure. Fearlessness comes not from the absence of challenges but from the knowledge that God is orchestrating a hopeful and purposeful future for you. How can you lean into God's promises and embrace a fearless attitude as you navigate life's uncertainties?

🗨 AFFIRMATION

I affirm my commitment to fearlessly forge futures in my leadership journey, guided by the promise of Jeremiah 29:11. I choose to trust in God's plans for me, knowing that He has thoughts of peace and a hopeful future in store. I believe that as I step out in faith and lead with courage, God will faithfully direct my path and empower me to impact lives and shape futures with loving purpose and passion.

🙏 PRAYER

Heavenly Father, thank You for the promise of a future filled with hope and purpose. Grant me the courage and faith to fearlessly trust in Your plans for me. Help me to lean into Your promises of peace and hope, knowing that You hold my future securely in Your hands. Guide me in leading with boldness, vision, and unwavering faith in Your providence. May Your will be done in my life as I step fearlessly into the future You have prepared for me. Amen.

NOTES

FEARLESS LEADERSHIP

> *Remember that I have told you this: Be strong and do not be afraid. Do not be weak but be brave. I, the Lord your God, will be with you, everywhere that you go. Joshua 1:9 (Easy)*

 DEVOTIONAL

Joshua 1:9 serves as a powerful reminder of God's command to be strong and courageous, knowing that He is always by your side. Strength and courage must be cultivated in those who desire to lead fearlessly. Don't be paralyzed by the fear of failure or of making mistakes. These moments may occur, but they are learning opportunities. They don't define your future. Take courage each day to be the best leader you can be. Trust that God is with you, helping you. Embrace this passage with unwavering faith, trusting in God's presence and guidance as you navigate the challenges and opportunities of leadership. Let this verse instill in you the confidence and boldness needed to lead with assurance and determination.

 PERSONAL APPLICATION

Leaders are required to execute many tasks. Whether it is giving a presentation at the department meeting, delivering a message at your church group, or preparing for an employment interview, it is normal to feel challenged and even fearful. Identify a leadership responsibility that intimidates you. Why do you find this task challenging? How can you approach it fearlessly, trusting in God's presence? Reflect on areas in your leadership journey where fear or discouragement may be holding you back from stepping into God's calling for your life. Consider how you can actively cultivate a spirit of strength and courage, leaning on God's promises and presence for support. Commit to embracing a mindset of bravery and trust in God's unfailing love as you lead with conviction and purpose.

🔍 REFLECTION

Consider moments when fear hindered your leadership.

- ✔ Was it the first day of class in a new school? Was it being new in the neighborhood, and you didn't know anyone? What about attending a new church for the first time? Or becoming a parent? How can you apply Joshua 1:9 in those situations?

- ✔ Reflect on the assurance of God's constant presence and command to be strong and courageous.

- ✔ Consider how this promise can shape your approach to leadership, empowering you to face challenges with confidence and resilience.

- ✔ How can you draw strength from God's presence and trust in His faithfulness as you fulfill your role as a leader?

🗨 AFFIRMATION

I affirm my commitment to embody strength and courage in my leadership journey, heeding the command of Joshua 1:9 with unwavering faith. I choose to cast aside fear and discouragement, trusting in God's presence and guidance wherever I go. I believe that as I walk in boldness and assurance, God will equip me to lead with purpose, impact lives, and fulfill His plans for me.

🙏 PRAYER

Heavenly Father, thank You for the command to be strong and courageous as Joshua 1:9 instructs. Grant me the strength and courage to face both large and small challenges with unwavering faith, knowing that You are with me every step of the way. Help me to overcome fear and discouragement, leaning on Your presence and promises for guidance and support. May Your unfailing love embolden me to lead with confidence and conviction, making a positive impact in the lives of those I serve. In Your mighty name, I pray. Amen.

NOTES

FOCUSED ON ETERNITY

> *We don't focus our attention on what is seen but on what is unseen. For what is seen is temporary, but the unseen realm is eternal. 2 Corinthians 4:18 (TPT)*

MEMORY SCRIPTURE

 DEVOTIONAL

The verse in 2 Corinthians 4:18 reminds you to set your sights on the eternal rather than the temporary. We are bombarded daily with commercials, ads, television shows, and other forms of entertainment that focus on temporary rewards. Temporal things belong to time and pass away. Eternal things are forever. Too often we drive ourselves toward what the world calls success at the cost of keeping our eyes and hearts away from things that really matter, the parts of us that belong to Eternity. Our leadership should exemplify a perspective that honors God. Embrace a perspective that values what is unseen and lasting, guiding your leadership decisions and actions with a focus on eternal significance. Let this scripture inspire you to lead with a vision that transcends the present moment, anchored in the hope of eternity.

 PERSONAL APPLICATION

Reflect on how you can align your leadership priorities with the eternal perspective presented in 2 Corinthians 4:18.

Have responsibilities and the pursuit of success shifted your perspective from the eternal to things that are temporary? Being successful in your career, signing a new client, having a big house, etc., are great, but they are not the only things that matter. Consider areas in your life and leadership where you may need to refocus on what truly matters. Commit to investing your time, energy, and resources in endeavors that have lasting impact beyond the temporal, leading with a sense of purpose and legacy that reflects eternal values.

🔍 REFLECTION

What does eternal mean to you? Think deeply about it and consider the impact of an eternal perspective on your decision-making.

✔ How can it bring purpose and meaning to your actions?

✔ Reflect on the contrast between the temporary and eternal as emphasized in 2 Corinthians 4:18. Contemplate how embracing an eternal perspective can shape your leadership approach and influence the way you make decisions.

✔ How can focusing on what is unseen and eternal guide you to lead in the temporal world with wisdom, integrity, and a commitment to advancing God's kingdom in all you do?

💬 AFFIRMATION

: I affirm my commitment to lead with a focus on eternity, guided by the truth of 2 Corinthians 4:18. I choose to fix my gaze on what is unseen and eternal, recognizing the fleeting nature of worldly pursuits. I believe that as I am anchored in eternal values and priorities, my actions will bear fruit that lasts beyond this lifetime, impacting lives and glorifying God for eternity.

🙏 PRAYER

Heavenly Father, thank You for the reminder to set my eyes on what is unseen and eternal. Help me to lead with a focus on eternity, aligning my priorities with Your kingdom values and purposes. Grant me the wisdom and discernment to make decisions that have lasting significance, reflecting Your love and truth in all I do. May my leadership be a testimony of Your eternal grace and glory, impacting lives for Your kingdom. In Jesus' name, I pray. Amen.

FAITHFUL FRIENDSHIP

> *A dear friend will love you no matter what, and a family sticks together through all kinds of trouble. Proverbs 17:17 (TPT)*

MEMORY SCRIPTURE

 DEVOTIONAL

The value of faithful friendships cannot be overstated. We were created for relationship with God and with others. Building friendships requires time and commitment. Focusing only on our career or education without considering friendships can create an emotional void within us. We must take every opportunity to cultivate strong, healthy friendships. Just as Proverbs 17:17 highlights the loyalty and support of a true friend, let us strive to cultivate and cherish such relationships in our lives. We each need a network of relationships that includes faithful friendships. We should endeavor to be faithful friends. Let us be intentional in being a loyal and supportive friend to those around us, reflecting the love and grace of Christ in our friendships.

 PERSONAL APPLICATION

Consider your friendships.

What is your shared history? Are they friends from childhood? The workplace? School? How do you regard your relationship with them? Today, I commit to being a faithful friend to those in my circle, offering my loyalty, support, and encouragement in times of need. I will share their joys and sorrows, their hopes, and fears. I will seek to cultivate deep and meaningful friendships built on trust, honesty, and mutual care. By embodying the qualities of a true friend, I aim to reflect the love of Christ in all my relationships.

REFLECTION

Take a moment to reflect on the friendships in your life.

- ✔ Are your friendships based on what they can do for you or what you can do for them, or are they based on mutual respect and love?
- ✔ Are there areas where you can be a more loyal and supportive friend?
- ✔ How can you strengthen the bonds of friendship through acts of kindness, understanding, and grace?
- ✔ Consider the impact of faithful friendships on your personal growth.

AFFIRMATION

I am grateful for the faithful friendships that surround me, and I am committed to being a loyal and supportive friend to others. I embrace the opportunity to reflect the love and compassion of Christ through my relationships, knowing that faithful friendships are a blessing and a source of strength in my life as a leader.

PRAYER

Dear Lord, thank you for the gift of faithful friendships that enrich our lives and support us in our journey. Help me to be a faithful and loyal friend to those around me, showing love, grace, and understanding in all my interactions. Help me to see potentially unhealthy relationships. Give me strength and courage to walk away from relationships that are taking me away from You. May my friendships reflect Your unconditional love and may they bring glory to Your name. Amen.

NOTES

____

____

____

ADDITIONAL NOTES

ADDITIONAL NOTES

GROW THROUGH GENEROSITY

> *Let giving flow from your heart, not from a sense of religious duty. Let it spring up freely from the joy of giving - all because God loves hilarious generosity! 2 Corinthians 9:7 (TPT)*

MEMORY SCRIPTURE

 DEVOTIONAL

Selfishness is the opposite of generosity. When we allow ourselves to become selfish and self-centered, we lose our Christ focus. Jesus gave himself to redeem us. He is generous in His love and mercy toward us, and as believers we must follow His example. Remember that your generosity is not just about material possessions but about sharing the love and blessings God has given you. Embrace the joy of giving wholeheartedly, knowing that God delights in those who give generously and cheerfully. Let your acts of generosity reflect the gladness of your faith and be a source of inspiration to others.

 PERSONAL APPLICATION

Today, choose to be a channel of God's blessings through your generous giving.

Too often we think of generosity as something financial and leave it at that. Generosity is so much more than that, and it's available to everyone. Another word for it might be loving-kindness. Be intentional about looking for those with whom you can generously share a smile, a kind word, a cup of coffee, a funny joke, or heartfelt companionship in joy or sorrow. Generosity occurs when we give something-not only when we give to someone else but also when we are willing to give the gift of generosity to ourselves. Holding yourself to rigid standards or being harsh with yourself is not generous. Give with a joyful heart, knowing that every act of generosity plants seeds of love, kindness, and hope in the lives of yourself and others. Commit to trusting in God's provision and stepping out in faith to bless those around you through your generosity.

 REFLECTION

Consider the times when you have experienced the joy of giving and its impact on both the giver and the recipient.

- ✔ How can you cultivate a mindset of abundance and generosity?
- ✔ In what ways can you encourage and inspire others to embrace the spirit of cheerful giving and share the glorious abundance of God's love through acts of generosity?

 AFFIRMATION

I am a vessel of God's love and generosity, and through my cheerful giving, I sow seeds of hope, joy, and compassion in the lives of myself and others. I trust in God's provision and abundance, knowing that He blesses those who give with a joyful heart. As a leader, I choose to flourish through faithful generosity, spreading God's love and light wherever I go.

PRAYER

Heavenly Father, thank you for Your endless blessings and love that inspire us to give generously and joyfully. Help me, Lord, to be a faithful steward of the resources and gifts You have entrusted to me. May my acts of generosity shine Your light and touch hearts, bringing glory to Your name. Amen.

GRATITUDE IN ADVERSITY

> *Whatever may happen to you, continue to thank God. God wants you to do that because you belong to Christ. 1 Thessalonians 5:18 (Easy)*

MEMORY SCRIPTURE

 DEVOTIONAL

As a leader facing adversity, it can be easy to become discouraged or overwhelmed. However, God calls us to a different response—one of gratitude. Building a career, completing an educational goal, starting a family, or any dream you want to realize inevitably comes with adversity. Things happen in everyone's life that don't seem to make any sense at all. There are moments when we can't help feeling overwhelmed, and that's when gratitude offers a way through the bewildering pain. It is a difficult but indispensable characteristic that leaders must cultivate. We don't have to make sense of the pain, but we do need to hold onto the reality of God's love, even when the pain is too great for us to feel it. In the midst of difficult circumstances, we are reminded to always be thankful, knowing that this is the way God desires us to live in Christ Jesus. Gratitude in adversity not only shifts our perspective but also strengthens our faith and trust in God's provision and plan.

 PERSONAL APPLICATION

Today, choose to cultivate a spirit of gratitude, even in the face of adversity.

Gratitude is connected to joy and living and leading joyfully. Instead of focusing on the challenges and obstacles before you, shift your perspective to see the blessings and opportunities that exist even in difficult circumstances. Commit to practice thankfulness in all situations, trusting that God is working all things together for your good.

 REFLECTION

Reflect on a recent difficult situation or challenge you have faced.

- ✔ How did you respond initially?
- ✔ How might your perspective have changed if you had approached the situation with gratitude and thankfulness from the start?
- ✔ Consider the ways in which gratitude can bring about a shift in your mindset and outlook, even in the midst of adversity.
- ✔ Take time every day to express gratitude and thankfulness to God for His goodness.
- ✔ Next, be intentional about expressing gratitude to those who support you in your leadership.

AFFIRMATION

I am a leader who chooses gratitude in adversity. I will always be thankful, trusting in God's plan and provision for my life. Through a spirit of gratitude, I will find strength, peace, and joy, knowing that God is with me in all circumstances. I will look for opportunities to express gratitude and appreciation to those who support me in my leadership journey.

PRAYER

Dear God, thank you for the reminder to always be thankful, even in the midst of adversity. Help me cultivate a spirit of gratitude that transcends my circumstances and reflects my trust in You. May gratitude be my response in all situations, knowing that You are working all things together for my good. Strengthen me, Lord, to live in gratitude and thankfulness each day. Amen.

 NOTES

GOD'S GRACE IN WEAKNESS

> **"** *But he answered me, 'My grace is always more than enough for you, and my power finds its full expression through your weakness. So I will celebrate my weaknesses, for when I'm weak I sense more deeply the mighty power of Christ living in me. 2 Corinthians 12:9 (TPT)* **"**

MEMORY SCRIPTURE

 DEVOTIONAL

As a leader, it can be easy to feel the pressure to be strong, capable, and perfect in all aspects of life and leadership. The demands of leadership can be overwhelming. We find ourselves sometimes running out of energy or hitting the wall. This is how burnout occurs. God reminds us that His grace is sufficient for us, especially in our weakness. In moments of inadequacy and vulnerability, you have the opportunity to experience the fullness of God's power working through you. It is through your weaknesses that Christ's strength is made perfect.

 PERSONAL APPLICATION

Today, I will embrace my weaknesses and vulnerabilities, knowing that they are opportunities for God's grace and power to shine through.

Am I insisting upon impossible perfection and struggling to be self-sustaining rather than relying on God's grace? If I am, then instead of striving for perfection, I will humbly acknowledge my limitations and rely on God's strength to sustain me. I will allow His grace to work in and through me, trusting that His power is made perfect in my weakness.

 REFLECTION

Reflect on a time when you felt weak or inadequate in your leadership role.

- ✔ What seemingly impossible moments were confronting you?
- ✔ Were you willing to receive God's amazing grace, or were you intent on finding your own solutions in your own strength?
- ✔ How did God's grace sustain you during that season?
- ✔ Consider how your weaknesses can be a platform for God's power to be displayed.
- ✔ Embrace the truth that His grace is sufficient for you, even in moments of weakness.

 AFFIRMATION

I am a leader who finds strength in God's grace in my weaknesses. It is through these moments that Christ's power is made perfect in me. I surrender my weaknesses to God, trusting that His grace is more than enough to sustain me in all circumstances.

PRAYER

Dear Lord, thank you for your abundant grace that sustains me in my weakness. Help me to embrace my vulnerabilities and shortcomings, knowing that it is through them that Your power is revealed. When I feel weak, that is when Your grace is most needed. Fill me with Your strength and grace, that I may lead with humility and reliance on Your power. May Your grace be my source of strength and confidence in all that I do. Amen.

NOTES

____

____

____

____

____

____

HARNESS HUMAN POTENTIAL

> *But you are God's chosen treasure-priests who are kings, a spiritual "nation" set apart as God's devoted ones. He called you out of darkness to experience his marvelous light, and now he claims you as his very own. He did this so that you would broadcast his glorious wonders throughout the world. 1 Peter 2:9 (TPT)*

MEMORY SCRIPTURE

 DEVOTIONAL

You are chosen and set apart by God for a unique purpose. Before you were born, God endowed you with amazing potential. You are a precious treasure in His eyes, called to serve as both a priest and a king in His kingdom. You are more than the title on your door or the title you wear at your church. Embrace your identity as a leader who has been called out of darkness into the marvelous light of God's grace. You are called and designed to reveal Jesus to everyone around you. Recognize that you are claimed as God's very own, entrusted with the potential to make a significant impact in the world around you.

 PERSONAL APPLICATION

Today, reflect on the truth that you are God's chosen treasure, set apart for His purposes.

You have potential to accomplish the purpose for which God created you. Discovering His purpose for you and maximizing the potential that you have been given are vital to your effectiveness as a leader. Resist living in a careless and undisciplined way. Rather, choose to yield to God's plan and will and not as if you are still in the old darkness. When frustrating things happen, harness the ungodly potential that may try and overwhelm you. Instead, with a grateful heart, recognize the unique gifts and abilities that God has given you and trust His guidance. Approach your leadership role with confidence, joy, and humility, knowing that you are called to be a light in the darkness and to make a difference in the lives of those around you.

REFLECTION

Consider the ways in which you have seen God's hand at work in your life, guiding and shaping you for leadership.

- ✔ As a believer, how do you see God reshaping old ways of thinking about leadership that don't glorify Him?
- ✔ Reflect on the significance of being chosen by God as His treasure and the responsibility that comes with being set apart for His purposes.
- ✔ How can you harness your human potential to fulfill the calling God has placed on your life?

AFFIRMATION

I am God's chosen treasure, called to be a leader in His kingdom. I embrace my identity as a priest and king, set apart to serve as His devoted one. I will harness my human potential to shine His light and make a positive impact in the world around me.

PRAYER

Lord, thank you for choosing me as Your treasure and calling me into Your marvelous light. Help me to embrace my identity as a leader who is set apart for Your purposes. Guide me in harnessing the potential within me to serve You faithfully and make a difference in the lives of others. May Your light shine through me as I lead with humility, grace, and love. Amen.

NOTES

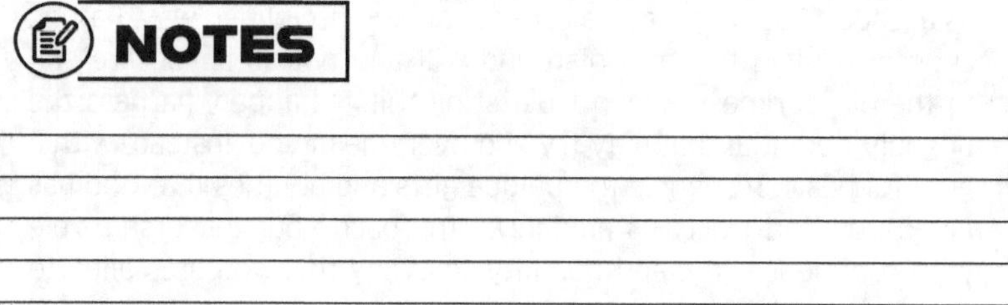

HUMILITY IN LEADERSHIP

MEMORY SCRIPTURE

 DEVOTIONAL

As a leader, it is important to cultivate humility. Arrogance and ego are forms of pride and are destructive leadership traits. Pride can lead to downfall and disgrace, but humility opens the door to wisdom and growth. True leadership is marked by a humble heart that is willing to learn, grow, and serve others with grace and compassion. We see this trait in the ministry of Jesus who was the best example of servant leadership. Embrace humility as a key virtue in your leadership style, knowing that it is through humility that true wisdom is gained.

PERSONAL APPLICATION

Today, I will reflect on areas in my leadership where pride may have taken root and hindered my growth.

Prideful leaders can create a toxic culture among those they lead and influence. I intentionally seek to cultivate humility in my interactions with others, listening with an open mind and learning from different perspectives. I will embrace opportunities to serve, to be a learner as well as a teacher, recognizing that the wisdom of true leadership is found in humility and grace. Humility honors the efforts and gifts of others, whereas pride honors only oneself. I will seek to honor God with all my heart and walk in humility as I lead others.

 REFLECTION

Consider a time when you witnessed humility in action and the impact it had on you and those around you.

- ✔ Consider an example from the leadership of Jesus and see how you can grow in this area of your life.
- ✔ Reflect on how pride may have hindered your growth or relationships in the past.
- ✔ How can you practice humility in your leadership role, allowing wisdom to guide your decisions and actions?
- ✔ Embrace the transformative power of humility in your leadership journey.

AFFIRMATION

I am a leader who embraces humility in my leadership. I choose to walk in humility, knowing that it leads to wisdom and growth. I will serve others with grace, compassion, and humility, seeking to learn from every opportunity and interaction. My leadership is marked by humility, and through it, I gain true wisdom.

PRAYER

Dear God, help me to follow the example of Jesus as I endeavor to walk in humility in my leadership journey. Teach me to set aside pride and embrace humility as a virtue that leads to wisdom and growth. Like Jesus, may I serve others with grace and compassion, learning from every experience and interaction. Guide me in leading with humility, knowing that true wisdom comes from a humble heart. Amen.

 NOTES

HOLY HABITS

> *Learn to live well in a way that makes God happy. 1 Timothy 4:7,8 (Easy)*

MEMORY SCRIPTURE

 DEVOTIONAL

As a leader, cultivating holy habits is essential for your spiritual growth and leadership development. This happens as we immerse ourselves in God's word, the Bible. Through consistent and diligent study of the Bible we learn what holy habits are. Submitting to God in prayer, study, and meditation each day is the key to cultivating holy habits. Commit to practices that align with God's Word and lead you closer to Him. Prioritize reading the Scriptures, encouraging fellow believers, and teaching them the truth. Let these habits shape your character and influence others to see your progress in faith.

 PERSONAL APPLICATION

Today, commit to cultivating holy habits in your daily life.

Prioritize reading and meditating on the Scriptures to deepen your understanding of God's truth. We are not transformed through self-effort but by submitting to the Holy Spirit. Difficult moments often reveal tendencies within us that must be laid aside. Not only must you develop personally and spiritually as a believer, but you must also seek opportunities to encourage and uplift your fellow believers, sharing the love and wisdom of Christ. Also dedicate time to teaching others, imparting the knowledge and insights you have gained from your own spiritual journey.

 REFLECTION

Reflect on the holy habits you currently practice in your life.

- ✔ How have these habits influenced your spiritual growth and leadership journey?
- ✔ Consider areas where you can further commit to cultivating practices that align with God's Word.
- ✔ Reflect on the impact these habits have on your relationship with God and others, and how they contribute to your progress in faith.

 AFFIRMATION

I am committed to cultivating holy habits in my life. Like a garden, my life requires careful pruning and weeding to eliminate the tangles and weeds that can grow within me. To accomplish this, I prioritize reading and meditating upon the Scriptures, talking to God in prayer, encouraging believers, and teaching them the good news of the Gospel. These practices shape my character and lead me closer to God. My commitment to holy habits reflects my progress in faith and inspires others to draw closer to Him, too.

 PRAYER

Lord, help me to cultivate holy habits that align with Your Word and draw me closer to You. Grant me the discipline and commitment to prioritize reading the Scriptures, encouraging fellow believers, and teaching them the truth. May these practices shape my character and lead me on a path of spiritual growth and leadership development. Guide me in living out these holy habits each day, that Your light may shine through me to others. Amen.

NOTES

____

____

____

HOLY SPIRIT-LED LIVING

MEMORY SCRIPTURE

 ## DEVOTIONAL

As a leader, the presence and guidance of the Holy Spirit are essential for navigating the challenges and opportunities that come your way. There are many influences vying for our attention every day. Many leaders have succumbed to influences that don't glorify God. Some depend on drugs, alcohol, and other addictive substances for their strength. For the Christian leader, the Spirit of Holiness, sent by the Father, is your strength. The Spirit of Holiness serves as your teacher and helper, leading you into truth and enabling you to remember the words of Jesus. John 14:26 reminds us that we have supernatural help from heaven. We can know how we are to live through God's word, the Bible, and through the indwelling Holy Spirit who is our teacher. Embrace a life of Holy Spirit-led living, allowing His wisdom and inspiration to guide your decisions and actions.

 ## PERSONAL APPLICATION

Today, open your heart to the leading of the Holy Spirit in all areas of your life.

You might experience stubborn areas that seem to hold you in their grip. If you seek the Holy Spirit's guidance and wisdom as you face them, they will lose their power over you. As you make decisions, face challenges, and interact with others, you will cultivate a spirit of receptivity to the teachings of the Holy Spirit, allowing His inspiration to shape your thoughts and actions. Walk in Holy Spirit-led living, trusting in His presence to guide you each step of the way.

REFLECTION

Reflect on a time when you felt the Holy Spirit leading and guiding you in a specific situation.

- ✔ How did His presence and wisdom impact your choices and outcomes?
- ✔ Consider areas in your life where you may need to be more attentive to the promptings of the Spirit and align your decisions with His guidance.
- ✔ Be consistent in submitting stubborn ungodly habits and ways of thinking to the Holy Spirit. As you do, you will experience the transformative power of Holy Spirit-led living in your leadership journey.

AFFIRMATION

I am a leader who embraces Holy Spirit-led living. I choose to resist the patterns of ungodly living. I trust in the guidance and wisdom of the Spirit of Holiness to lead me into truth and inspire me to remember the teachings of Jesus. I will walk in step with the Holy Spirit, allowing His presence to shape my decisions and actions for His glory.

PRAYER

Dear Holy Spirit, thank you for being my teacher and guide, leading me into truth and inspiring me to remember the words of Jesus. I invite Your presence to fill me afresh today and guide me in every aspect of my life and leadership. Help me to be attentive to Your promptings, receptive to Your teachings, and surrendered to Your will. May I walk in Holy Spirit-led living, bringing honor and glory to Your name. Amen.

INNOVATE WITH INTEGRITY

> **"**
> *Integrity will lead you to success, but treachery will destroy your dreams.*
> *Proverbs 11:3 (TPT)*
> **"**

MEMORY SCRIPTURE

 DEVOTIONAL

As a leader, it is essential to innovate with integrity, aligning your actions and decisions with honesty and moral principles. Many leaders fall prey to competitive schemes and tactics to gain promotion and recognition. Violating the principles that govern teamwork by taking sole credit for collaborative work or taking credit for another leader's work is not integral. This is also true if you cheat on a test or falsify reports to improve the ways others perceive you. Integrity is the cornerstone of success and happiness in leadership, guiding you to build trust, credibility, and a positive reputation. In a world that often values shortcuts and deceit, choose to uphold integrity as you strive to innovate and make a positive impact. If you maintain your integrity, you cannot go wrong, no matter what the world says.

 PERSONAL APPLICATION

Today, commit to leading with integrity in all aspects of your life and leadership.

Seek to innovate with honesty, transparency, and ethical conduct, ensuring that your actions reflect kingdom values and teachings. Prioritize integrity in your decision-making processes, even when you are faced with challenges or temptations that threaten to compromise your values. Commit to a way of integrity as you journey to success and happiness.

🔍 REFLECTION

Consider past temptations when you gave in and did not lead with integrity. How did you feel in those moments?

- ✔ Were the outcomes worth the violation of the principles of integrity?
- ✔ Reflect on a time when integrity played a significant role in a decision or action you took as a leader.
- ✔ How did upholding integrity impact the outcome and your relationships?
- ✔ Consider the importance of maintaining integrity in a world that often values success at any cost.
- ✔ Reflect on how you can innovate with integrity, staying true to kingdom values and principles.

💬 AFFIRMATION

I am a leader who innovates with integrity. I choose to uphold honesty, transparency, and ethical conduct in all my endeavors, knowing that integrity leads to success and happiness. I will build trust, credibility, and positive relationships through my commitment to integrity in leadership. My innovative spirit is guided by the principles of integrity. I will be sensitive to opportunities to innovate and collaborate with a team, and I will celebrate and acknowledge the efforts of those who innovate with me.

🙏 PRAYER

Dear God, grant me the strength and wisdom to lead with integrity in all that I do. Help me to innovate with honesty, transparency, and ethical conduct, reflecting Your values and principles in my leadership journey. Guard my heart against treachery, jealousy, and deceit, and guide me to make decisions that honor You and benefit others above all. May integrity be the cornerstone of my character, my success, and my happiness as a leader. Amen.

INTENTIONAL INTERCESSION

> *Confess and acknowledge how you have offended one another and then pray for one another to be instantly healed, for tremendous power is released through the passionate, heartfelt prayer of a godly believer!*
> *James 5:16 (TPT)*

MEMORY SCRIPTURE

 DEVOTIONAL

Conflict in a team is inevitable. Too often we only see our position, and we are sure that we are right. When there is tension and conflict, it is extremely easy for toxic feelings to build. Even Christian believers can find it difficult to release negative feelings and resentment. There is a way to resolve this, and that is to pray for those who are offending us. This is the practice of intentional intercession. Its immense power and significance help us to move beyond difficult moments as we fulfill the biblical instruction to pray for one another. When we confess our resentments and lift each other up in prayer, healing and restoration can flow into our relationships and circumstances. The passionate and heartfelt prayers of a godly believer have the ability to release tremendous power and bring about transformation. When you find yourself in a place of conflict, approach intercession with intentionality and faith, believing in the impact it can have on those around you.

 PERSONAL APPLICATION

Today, commit to intentional intercession in your life and leadership.

Take time to confess any offenses and seek reconciliation with others, understanding the importance of maintaining healthy relationships. Pray fervently for those around you, lifting up their needs, struggles, and joys before the Lord. Trust in the power of prayer to bring healing and transformation, both personally and in the lives of those you intercede for.

 REFLECTION

Reflect on the transformative power of intentional intercession in your life and leadership.

- ✔ Do you take time to pray for your family, team, workplace, etc.?
- ✔ Consider the times when prayer has brought about healing, reconciliation, and breakthrough.
- ✔ Reflect on the significance of confessing faults and praying for one another, recognizing the impact it can have on building strong, supportive relationships.
- ✔ How can you deepen your practice of intentional intercession?

 AFFIRMATION

I commit to intentional intercession. I believe in the power of passionate and heartfelt prayer to bring healing, transformation, and breakthrough for myself and others. I will confess my faults, seek reconciliation, and lift others up in prayer, trusting in the tremendous power released through intercession. My prayers are impactful and effective in the lives of those I intercede for.

 PRAYER

Lord, thank you for the gift of intercession and the power of prayer. Your word, the Bible, tells me that Jesus is seated at the right hand of the Father interceding for me. Help me to follow the example of Jesus and approach intentional intercession with sincerity, passion, and faith. Teach me to confess my faults, seek reconciliation, and fervently pray for those around me. May my prayers be a source of healing, transformation, and blessing in the lives of others. Strengthen my faith in the power of intercession and guide me to be a godly believer who impacts the world through prayer. Amen.

 NOTES

INTEGRITY IN LEADERSHIP

"

Above all, set yourself apart as a model of a life nobly lived. With dignity, demonstrate integrity in all that you teach. Titus 2:7-8 (TPT)

"

MEMORY SCRIPTURE

 ## DEVOTIONAL

As a leader, integrity is a foundational quality that sets you apart and influences those around you. A lack of integrity greatly diminishes your capacity to lead others as you are perceived as being untrustworthy. Inconsistent behavior that does not reflect biblical values impedes your progress and the progress of those connected to you. The decisions you make daily must reflect biblical values, which include integrity. Be a leader who speaks with honesty and consistency, reflecting the values you teach through your actions. Let your integrity shine through in every aspect of your leadership, guiding others with authenticity and trustworthiness. Uphold the standard of integrity in all you do, knowing that your example speaks volumes to those in your care.

 ## PERSONAL APPLICATION

Today, strive to embody integrity in your leadership role.

Speak with honesty and consistency, aligning your words with your actions. Remember, it may seem easier to deviate from the path of integrity or to take shortcuts at the expense of others to achieve success. The end result is never worth it because you become less than the person God made you. Let everything you do reflect the values and teachings the Bible upholds, demonstrating integrity and seriousness in your leadership. Allow your commitment to integrity to inspire trust and respect among those you lead.

REFLECTION

Reflect on the importance of integrity in leadership and the impact it has on those around you.

- ✔ Consider how not only your words but, more importantly, your actions align with the values you profess to uphold. How do you see integrity in the life and ministry of Jesus?
- ✔ Reflect on areas where you can further demonstrate integrity and consistency in your leadership role.
- ✔ How can your example influence others to see the value of walking the path of integrity and trustworthiness?

AFFIRMATION

I am a leader committed to integrity in leadership. I speak with honesty and consistency, reflecting the values I teach through my actions. I will avoid jealousy, gossip, and slander, which damage my integrity. My integrity shines through in all I do, guiding others with authenticity and trustworthiness. I uphold the standard of integrity, knowing that my example inspires respect and trust among those I lead.

PRAYER

Holy Spirit, help me to lead with integrity and authenticity in all aspects of my life and leadership. Grant me the strength to speak with honesty and consistency, aligning my words with my actions. May everything I do reflect the values and teachings I uphold, demonstrating integrity and seriousness in my leadership role. Guide me in setting an example of trustworthiness and authenticity for those under my care. Amen.

NOTES

____

____

____

ADDITIONAL NOTES

ADDITIONAL NOTES

JOURNEY WITH JOY

> You will lead me along the path of life. Because you are with me, I am very happy. I know that I will be with you forever, and that makes me very happy! Psalm 16:11 (TPT)

MEMORY SCRIPTURE

 DEVOTIONAL

Your journey is filled with opportunities, challenges, and growth. For many leaders, depression and other forms of emotional distress can be all too common. The constant demand to perform well, to be invincible, can be overwhelming. The stress of performance, getting it right every time, robs you of joy. In the midst of setbacks, mistakes, job pressures, and the separate demands of your personal life, God invites you to walk in His presence, where fullness of joy is found. When you seek His guidance and abide in His love, you discover that joy is not dependent on circumstances but flows from the depths of your relationship with Him. Embrace the path of life with joy as your constant companion, knowing that in God's presence, there are pleasures forevermore.

 PERSONAL APPLICATION

Choosing to journey with joy each day requires you to become dependent upon God's strength and power. You may not have all the answers, but He does.

In His presence is fullness of joy. Let it overflow into your relationship with Him and with others. It is your strength. Endeavor to seek God's presence in every aspect of your life, knowing that true joy is found in Him. Approach challenges with a spirit of joy, trusting in His guidance and provision. Through prayer and worship, cultivate a heart of gratitude and praise, recognizing the blessings that surround you. May joy be your strength and your source of resilience as you navigate the path of life.

REFLECTION

Are you overwhelmed today?

- ✔ What issues are stealing your joy?
- ✔ How are you meeting them?
- ✔ With resistance or with joyful assurance?
- ✔ Reflect on moments in your leadership journey where you have experienced the fullness of joy in God's presence.
- ✔ Consider how joy has impacted your perspective, attitudes, and interactions with others.
- ✔ Reflect on the difference between worldly happiness and the deep, abiding joy that comes from walking closely with God.
- ✔ How can you cultivate a spirit of joy in your leadership role today?

AFFIRMATION

I am a leader who journeys with joy in God's presence. I embrace the path of life with a heart filled with gratitude, praise, and resilience. Each day I will take notice of the small things God is doing for me, and I will be joyful. In His presence, I find fullness of joy that sustains me through challenges and blessings alike. I choose to walk in joy, knowing that at His right hand are pleasures forevermore.

PRAYER

Dear Lord, thank you for the gift of joy that comes from walking in Your presence. Help me to journey with joy, finding strength and resilience in Your love. May my heart be filled with gratitude and praise, knowing that true joy is found in You alone. Guide me on the path of life, and may Your presence be my constant source of joy and pleasure. Amen.

NOTES

JOYFUL PRAISE

The Lord makes me strong. He keeps me safe like a shield. I trust in him completely, and he has helped me. I am very happy, and I will thank him with my songs. Psalm 28:7 (TPT)

MEMORY SCRIPTURE

DEVOTIONAL

It is important to find strength and protection in God, trusting fully in His provision and care. Joy is more than a smile on your face. Joy springs forth from within, like a stream of living water, and nothing can stop its flow. Let your words and actions, your whole way of living, ring out your joy! Joy takes us beyond our current situation or crisis to a place where we gaze upon God's heavenly face. Though it can happen in the smallest, most insignificant ways, it is real. When things become difficult, we can be tempted to murmur and complain, blame others, and feel sorry for ourselves. Resist the urge! Instead, choose to honor God with joyful praise, even if you don't feel joyful. When you lean on Him with unwavering faith, His help is on its way to guide and support you. Let your heart overflow with joy and praise, expressing gratitude for all that God is to you. Sing songs of His goodness and faithfulness, celebrating His presence in your life and leadership journey.

PERSONAL APPLICATION

Anchor your trust in God as your strength and shield, knowing that He is your help in times of need.

If you cultivate a heart of joyful praise that bursts forth with gratitude and adoration for His faithfulness, you will overcome the weariness that overwhelms many leaders and causes them to doubt their calling. Express your love for God through songs of worship, declaring His significance in your life and leadership. Whistle a happy tune, lift up your hands in adoration unto God and watch the clouds of despair begin to fade away. Let the sound of praises reflect the joy and gratitude that fill your heart.

REFLECTION

Reflect on the ways in which God has been your strength and shield in challenging times.

- ✔ Consider moments when His help was evident as you trusted in His provision.
- ✔ Reflect on the joy and gratitude that arise from a heart filled with praise for God's goodness and faithfulness.
- ✔ How can you incorporate joyful praise into your leadership role, celebrating God's presence and guidance in every aspect of your life?

AFFIRMATION

I am a leader who finds strength and protection in God. I trust in His provision, knowing that help is on the way when I lean on Him with unwavering faith. My heart overflows with joyful praise, bursting forth with gratitude and adoration for His faithfulness. I will sing songs of worship, declaring the significance of God in my life.

PRAYER

Dear God, thank you for being my strength and shield in every circumstance. Help me to trust in Your provision and care, knowing that You are my help in times of need. Fill my heart with joyful praise, overflowing with gratitude and adoration for Your faithfulness. May my songs of worship reflect the joy and gratitude that fill my heart, celebrating Your presence and guidance in my life and leadership. Amen.

NOTES

KINDLE KNOWLEDGE AND KINDNESS

> *If you want to know how to live in a good way, you must first learn to respect the Lord with fear. Fools refuse to listen to wise teachings.*
> Proverbs 1:7 (TPT)

MEMORY SCRIPTURE

 DEVOTIONAL

The pursuit of wisdom and knowledge is essential for your growth and effectiveness in leadership. True wisdom begins with a heart devoted to God, seeking obedience and alignment with His will. This is a fire that you must rekindle each day. Ego and vanity have no place in a leader's life. They put the image of self in place of God's image and only succeed in impacting a leader's influence in a negative way. Remember that the wisdom of loving-kindness always points to God. A kind word spoken at the right moment can help someone see their own value. And when someone points out something you yourself have overlooked, respond with humility and gratitude. It will reveal the humility of Jesus at work in your heart. Embrace a posture of humility and openness to learning, recognizing that true knowledge comes from a place of surrender to God's guidance. Avoid the trap of pride and self-sufficiency that hinders the acquisition of wisdom, and instead cultivate a spirit of obedience and devotion to God.

 PERSONAL APPLICATION

Today, prioritize the pursuit of wisdom through living in obedient devotion to God.

You don't always have to be the one with the answer. Allow others to shine. Acknowledge their efforts and knowledge. Humbly seek knowledge and understanding, recognizing that true wisdom is found in surrendering to His guidance. Guard against the temptation of pride and self-sufficiency, choosing instead to embrace a posture of humility and openness to learning. Let your pursuit of knowledge be rooted in a deep devotion to God, seeking His wisdom to guide you in your leadership journey.

🔍 REFLECTION

Reflect on your approach to seeking wisdom and knowledge in your leadership role.

- ✔ Consider how your devotion to God impacts your pursuit of wisdom and understanding.
- ✔ Engage in a learning activity and perform a random act of kindness.
- ✔ Reflect on how the combination of knowledge and kindness enriches your life and the lives of those around you.
- ✔ Reflect on areas where pride or self-sufficiency may hinder your growth in wisdom.
- ✔ How can you cultivate a spirit of humility and obedience to God, allowing Him to guide you in acquiring true knowledge?

AFFIRMATION

I am a leader committed to kindling knowledge and kindness in my life and leadership. I prioritize obedience and devotion to God as the foundation of true wisdom. I choose humility and openness to learning, seeking knowledge that aligns with His will. My pursuit of wisdom is rooted in a deep desire to grow in understanding and effectiveness as a leader.

🙏 PRAYER

Dear God, guide me in the pursuit of wisdom and knowledge. Help me to live in obedient devotion to You, seeking Your guidance and wisdom in all that I do. Grant me a spirit of humility and openness to learning, guarding me against pride and self-sufficiency. May my pursuit of knowledge be rooted in a deep love for You, seeking Your wisdom to lead with kindness and understanding. Amen.

KINGDOM-MINDED LEADERSHIP

> *Instead, always think about the things that are important in the kingdom of heaven. Always do what God shows you is right. Then he will also give you the things that you need each day.*
> Matthew 6:33 (TPT)

 DEVOTIONAL

It is crucial to prioritize a kingdom-minded approach to leadership. Jesus instructs us to seek first the kingdom of God and His righteousness, trusting that all other things will fall into place. Although dreams and aspirations of promotion and recognition can be admirable, your pursuit of them must always reflect kingdom values. We cannot be blinded by the glory of visibility or the accolades of men. Recognition and promotion are commendable but never at the expense of our kingdom identity. Kingdom-minded leadership places God's purposes and principles at the forefront, aligning our actions and decisions with His will. By chasing after the realm of God's kingdom instead of the world, we set the foundation for effective and impactful leadership that glorifies Him. That is the way to bring His kingdom into the world.

 PERSONAL APPLICATION

Commit to being a kingdom-minded leader by seeking first the realm of God's kingdom and His righteousness.

Prioritize aligning your leadership with God's will, trusting that He will provide abundantly for all your needs. Seek to lead with integrity, compassion, and wisdom, reflecting the values of God's kingdom in all aspects of your leadership. May your focus on the kingdom of God guide you in making decisions that honor Him and benefit those under your care.

REFLECTION

Reflect on your leadership approach and priorities.

- ✔ Consider how you currently integrate kingdom principles into your leadership style.

- ✔ Reflect on areas where you can better align your leadership with God's kingdom and righteousness.

- ✔ Evaluate your priorities. How can you ensure your leadership aligns with seeking God's kingdom first?

- ✔ How can a kingdom-minded focus enhance your effectiveness and impact as a leader?

AFFIRMATION

I am committed to kingdom-minded leadership. I prioritize seeking God's kingdom and righteousness above all else, trusting in His provision and guidance. My leadership is rooted in integrity, compassion, and wisdom, reflecting the values of God's kingdom in all that I do. I embrace a kingdom-minded approach to leadership, knowing that it brings honor to God and blessings to those I lead.

PRAYER

Lord, guide me in cultivating a kingdom-minded approach to leadership. Help me to seek first Your kingdom and righteousness in all my decisions and actions, placing your will above my own. Grant me wisdom and discernment to lead with integrity and compassion, reflecting Your values in my leadership. May my focus on Your kingdom bring glory to Your name and blessings to those I lead. Amen.

NOTES

____

____

____

LEAD WITH LOVE AND LEARN

> *Until then, there are three things that remain: faith, hope, and love—yet love surpasses them all. So above all else, let love be the beautiful prize for which you run.*
> 1 Corinthians 13:13 (TPT)

MEMORY SCRIPTURE

 ## DEVOTIONAL

Love is the cornerstone of effective leadership. Endeavoring to lead from a heart of love is a powerful catalyst for developing servant leadership. The apostle Paul reminds us that faith, hope, and love are enduring virtues, but love surpasses them all. These three virtues must be our motivations. The exaltation of ourselves has nothing to do with faith or hope, and certainly not with love. Leading with love involves compassion, kindness, and understanding. Love motivates us to serve selflessly, listen attentively, and empathize deeply with others. Let love be the guiding principle in your leadership journey, inspiring trust, unity, and growth within your team.

 ## PERSONAL APPLICATION

Today, like Jesus, strive to lead with love as your guiding principle.

Seek opportunities to show compassion, kindness, and understanding. Listen attentively, serve selflessly, and empathize deeply with the needs of others. Commit to making love the foundation of your leadership style, knowing that it fosters trust, unity, and growth within your circle of influence. May love be the driving force in all your interactions and decisions as a leader.

REFLECTION

Reflect on the role of love in your leadership style.

- ✔ Consider how you currently demonstrate compassion, kindness, and understanding towards others.
- ✔ How do you see these characteristics in Jesus, the Leader?
- ✔ Reflect on the impact that leading with love can have on building trust, unity, and growth within your team.
- ✔ How can you prioritize love as the guiding principle in your leadership journey?

AFFIRMATION

I am committed to leading with love and learning from those I serve. Love is the foundation of my leadership style, inspiring compassion, kindness, and understanding in all my interactions. I strive to serve selflessly, listen attentively, and empathize deeply with the needs of others. Love guides me in fostering trust, unity, and growth with those I influence, making it the beautiful prize for which I run.

PRAYER

Dear God, teach me to lead with love as my guiding principle in all aspects of my leadership journey. Help me to follow the example of Jesus to show compassion, kindness, and understanding towards those I influence, reflecting Your love in my interactions. Grant me the wisdom to serve selflessly, listen attentively, and empathize deeply with the needs of others. May love be the driving force behind my leadership, fostering trust, unity, and growth. Amen.

NOTES

LOVE AS A LIFESTYLE

> *Let love and kindness be the motivation behind all that you do. 1 Corinthians 16:14 (TPT)*

MEMORY SCRIPTURE

DEVOTIONAL

In yesterday's devotional we discovered how to lead with love and to learn as we lead. This requires you to embrace love as a lifestyle. This is a powerful way to impact those around you. The simple yet profound command in 1 Corinthians 16:14 reminds us to infuse every aspect of our lives and leadership with love. Love should be the driving force behind our words, actions, and decisions. Let love be the guiding principle that shapes your interactions and relationships.

PERSONAL APPLICATION

Within our circles of leadership there is usually someone who requires more time, patience, love, tolerance, etc.

We don't naturally display the necessary love characteristics toward someone like that. It's easier to be impatient and scornful, push them away, or neglect them. It helps to remember what Jesus taught in Matthew 25:40: "When you cared for one of the least of these, my little ones, my true brothers and sisters, you demonstrated love for me" (TPT). To meet these difficult brothers and sisters with love requires reliance on the Holy Spirit.

Today, commit to following the example of Jesus and make love your lifestyle. Strive to do everything in love, showing kindness, compassion, patience, and above all, grace to those around you. Seek opportunities to demonstrate love in your words, actions, and decisions, fostering a positive and supportive environment. Choose to lead with love as a lifestyle, knowing that it has the power to transform hearts and inspire greatness in others.

 REFLECTION

Reflect on the significance of making love your lifestyle as a leader.

- ✔ How did Jesus express love to those who followed him?
- ✔ Consider how you currently express love, kindness, and compassion in your leadership role.
- ✔ Reflect on the impact that leading with love can have on building trust, respect, and unity with the people you influence.
- ✔ As a leader, if you model these traits, they positively affect the culture in which you live and lead. How can you cultivate a culture of love that influences your lifestyle and interactions with others?

AFFIRMATION

I am dedicated to living out love as a lifestyle. Love guides my words, actions, and decisions, shaping my interactions with others. I choose to show kindness, compassion, and grace in all circumstances, fostering a culture of respect and unity within my team. Love is the foundation of my lifestyle, inspiring greatness, and transformation in those I influence.

PRAYER

Dear God, help me to embrace love as a lifestyle in my leadership journey. Grant me the strength and wisdom to do everything in love, showing kindness, compassion, and grace to those around me. I pray that love will be the driving force behind my words, actions, and decisions, creating a positive and supportive environment for those around me. Help me to be an example of the way in which Jesus loved and led. Holy Spirit, guide me in cultivating a culture of love that reflects Your heart and transforms lives. Amen.

LISTENING TO GOD'S VOICE

> *When you turn to the right or turn to the left,*
> *you will hear his voice behind you to guide you,*
> *saying, "This is the right path, follow it."*
> *Isaiah 30:21 (TPT)*

 DEVOTIONAL

Learning to listen to God's voice is essential for navigating the complexities of leadership. There are so many responsibilities and challenges each day. We can become so anxious and overwhelmed that we respond in sharp words or grow distracted when others are speaking to us. While they are speaking to us, our minds are drifting away toward something else. Multi-tasking, which many leaders feel compelled to do, can actually create more stress and distraction. In these moments, we can miss the still, small voice of the Lord speaking to us in our hearts. Isaiah 30:21 reminds us that God guides us with His voice, directing us on the right path. How can we hear His voice if we are not listening for it? Amidst the noise and distractions of the world, God's voice speaks with clarity and wisdom, leading us in the way we should go. Find time daily to quiet your heart and mind, listening for God's gentle whisper that points you in the direction of His purpose for your life and leadership.

 PERSONAL APPLICATION

Today, commit to listening to God's voice as a you lead.

Create space for quiet reflection and prayer, seeking to hear His guidance and direction. Pay attention to the nudges of the Holy Spirit, trusting that God will lead you on the right path. Choose to tune out the distractions of the world and tune in to the still, small voice of God, allowing His wisdom to guide your decisions and actions.

REFLECTION

God speaks to us all the time. Sometimes words or phrases suddenly echo in our minds, and other times a feeling of rightness or a vision of goodness fills our hearts. If we are listening, we will recognize God's voice in these moments. Consider how you discern God's guidance amidst the busyness of life.

- ✔ Reflect on your current practice of listening to God's voice.
- ✔ Recall a time when you realized later that you had heard the still, small voice of God, but somehow in the moment, you didn't recognize that it was God speaking.
- ✔ Reflect on moments when you felt led by God's voice in your decision-making process.
- ✔ How can you create intentional space to listen for His voice and follow His direction in your leadership role?

AFFIRMATION

I am tuned to the frequency of God's voice, seeking His guidance and wisdom in all aspects of my leadership journey. I choose to listen for His direction, trusting that He will lead me on the right path. I tune out distractions and tune in to the still, small voice of God, allowing His guidance to shape my decisions and actions as a leader.

PRAYER

Lord, open my ears and heart to listen to Your voice. Help me to discern Your guidance amidst the noise of the world, seeking Your wisdom in all my decisions and actions. May Your voice lead me on the right path, guiding me in fulfilling Your purpose for my life and leadership. Grant me the courage and faith to follow Your direction with trust and obedience. Amen.

NOTES

____

____

____

Motivate and Master Challenges

> *I am trained in the secret of overcoming all things, whether in fullness or in hunger. And I find that the strength of Christ's explosive power infuses me to conquer every difficulty."*
> Philippians 4:13 (TPT)

MEMORY SCRIPTURE

 DEVOTIONAL

All leaders face challenges and obstacles along their leadership journey. However, the promise in Philippians 4:13 reminds us that we have access to Christ's strength and power to overcome any difficulty that comes our way. Rather than being discouraged by challenges, let them motivate you to grow, learn, and become a stronger leader. Embrace each obstacle as an opportunity to rely on Christ's strength and conquer whatever stands in your path.

 PERSONAL APPLICATION

What challenges are you facing? Have you submitted those challenges to the Lord?

Approach challenges with a mindset of motivation and mastery. Remember that Christ's power is within you, empowering you to conquer every difficulty that arises. View challenges as opportunities for growth and learning, trusting that each obstacle you face is a chance to rely on Christ's strength. Commit to facing challenges with courage, determination, and faith, knowing that you can overcome them through the power of Christ.

 REFLECTION

Consider how you have responded to difficulties in the past.

- ✔ Reflect on the challenges you have encountered in your leadership role.
- ✔ Reflect on times when you have felt Christ's strength empowering you to overcome obstacles.
- ✔ How can you view challenges as opportunities for growth and rely on Christ's strength to help you master them?
- ✔ Watch for opportunities to share words of encouragement with someone facing a challenge.
- ✔ How did mastering your own challenges and being a source of motivation for others bring you a sense of purpose?
- ✔ Take Jesus for your model. How did He face the challenges that confronted Him in His life and ministry? How did He motivate others?

AFFIRMATION

I am empowered by Christ's strength to conquer challenges. I face difficulties with courage, determination, and faith, knowing that His power infuses me to overcome every obstacle. Challenges motivate me to grow, learn, and become a stronger leader. I embrace each difficulty as an opportunity to rely on Christ's strength and master whatever comes my way.

PRAYER

Dear Lord, thank you for the promise of Your strength and power to help me conquer challenges. Empower me with Your explosive power to face difficulties with courage and faith. Help me view challenges as opportunities for growth and learning, relying on Your strength to guide me through every obstacle. May Your power infuse me with motivation so that I can master my doubt and fear and overcome any difficulty that comes my way. Amen.

MIND RENEWAL

> *Stop imitating the ideals and opinions of the culture around you but be inwardly transformed by the Holy Spirit through a total reformation of how you think. This will empower you to discern God's will as you live a beautiful life, satisfying and perfect in his eyes. Romans 12:2 (TPT)*

MEMORY SCRIPTURE

 DEVOTIONAL

The process of mind renewal is crucial for aligning your thoughts and perspectives with God's will. Romans 12:2 calls us to break away from the patterns of the world and allow the Holy Spirit to transform our minds. We accomplish this when we submit our thoughts and desires to the Lord. This is when we gain Heaven's perspective. Before we became new creations in Christ, our thoughts and desires were aligned with darkness. By renewing our thinking, we gain clarity and discernment to understand God's perfect will for our lives and leadership. Embrace the journey of mind renewal as a means to live a life that reflects God's beauty, satisfaction, and perfection.

 PERSONAL APPLICATION

Today, commit to the journey of mind renewal. As you do, you will intentionally break away from worldly influences and allow the Holy Spirit to transform your thought patterns.

Seek to align your thinking with God's Word and His will, trusting that this renewal process will empower you to discern His perfect plan for your life and leadership. Choose to embrace a mindset that reflects God's beauty, satisfaction, and perfection.

🔍 REFLECTION

Reflect on the current state of your thought patterns and perspectives as a leader.

- ✔ Consider the influences that shape your thinking on a daily basis.
- ✔ Reflect on areas where your mindset may need renewal and alignment with God's will.
- ✔ Identify a worldly mindset you need to surrender. How can you actively renew your mind according to God's Word?
- ✔ How can you actively engage in the process of mind renewal to gain clarity and discernment?

💬 AFFIRMATION

I am a leader committed to the journey of mind renewal. I choose to break away from worldly influences and allow the Holy Spirit to transform my thinking. My mind is renewed to align with God's will and Word, empowering me to discern His perfect plan for my life and leadership. I embrace a mindset that reflects God's beauty, satisfaction, and perfection, guiding me in all aspects of my life and leadership.

🙏 PRAYER

Dear Lord, guide me on the path of mind renewal. Help me break away from the patterns of the world and allow Your Spirit to transform my thoughts. Renew my mind to align with Your will and Word, empowering me to discern Your perfect plan for my life and leadership. May my renewed mindset reflect Your beauty, satisfaction, and perfection in all that I do. Amen.

✍️ NOTES

MISSION-MINDED LIVING

> **"** Now wherever you go, make disciples of all nations, baptizing them in the name of the Father, the Son, and the Holy Spirit. And teach them to faithfully follow all that I have commanded you. And never forget that I am with you, every day, even to the completion of this age. Matthew 28:19-20 (TPT) **"**

MEMORY SCRIPTURE

DEVOTIONAL

Leaders are called to live a mission-minded life dedicated to making disciples and spreading the message of Christ. The Great Commission in Matthew 28:19-20 urges us to go out, baptize, make disciples, and teach others the ways of Jesus. There are possibilities each day for us to engage in the mission of Heaven. Lost souls are looking for Jesus our Redeemer, and often they don't know where or how to find Him. They end up looking in strange places, like addictions, where all they find is suffering. As a believer you are a messenger. You carry the message of the Good News that Jesus lives and wants everyone, great and small, lost and found, to enter His kingdom. Embrace this mission as a central focus of your leadership journey. Let the passion for sharing the love of Christ motivate you to impact lives and fulfill the calling to make disciples of all nations.

PERSONAL APPLICATION

Today, commit to living a mission-minded life by actively seeking opportunities to share the message of Christ with others and make disciples for Him.

Engage in the process of teaching and discipling individuals, showing them the ways of Jesus through your actions and words. Fill your heart and mind with God's word so that you are confident in sharing the Good News with others. Choose to live out the Great Commission in your daily life, knowing that God's presence will be with you every step of the way.

REFLECTION

Reflect on the significance of the Great Commission in your leadership role.

- ✔ Consider how you can actively engage in making disciples and spreading the message of Christ.
- ✔ Our mission assignment is not silent; we must tell others the good news. Reflect on the impact of living a mission-minded life.
- ✔ How can you align your actions and decisions with the call to fulfill the Great Commission in all aspects of your life?

AFFIRMATION

I am a leader committed to living a mission-minded life. I embrace the call to make disciples, baptize, and teach others the ways of Jesus. My passion for sharing the love of Christ motivates me to impact lives and fulfill the Great Commission. I choose to be a vessel of God's love and truth, knowing that His presence will guide me in my mission-minded living.

PRAYER

Holy Spirit, empower me to live a mission-minded life. Give me the courage and passion to make disciples, baptize, and teach others the ways of Jesus. Help me to fulfill the Great Commission with faith and obedience, knowing that Your presence is with me always. May my life reflect Your love and truth as I strive to impact lives and spread Your message to all nations. Amen.

NOTES

✎ ADDITIONAL NOTES

ADDITIONAL NOTES

Nurture New Narratives

> *Keep your thoughts continually fixed on all that is authentic and real, honorable and admirable, beautiful and respectful, pure and holy, merciful and kind. And fasten your thoughts on every glorious work of God, praising him always.*
> Philippians 4:8 (TPT)

MEMORY SCRIPTURE

 ## DEVOTIONAL

The narratives we nurture in our minds shape our perspectives, attitudes, and actions. Leaders are not exempt from the challenges of inappropriate thoughts, which then lead to inappropriate actions. The messages of contemporary culture encourage a world view where people who make their own way and are out for themselves are considered admirable and strong. The value of community and mutuality takes a much lower place. The emphasis on self-determination and self-realization infiltrates our patterns of living unless we overcome them through yielding to God's ways. Philippians 4:8 encourages us to focus on thoughts that are authentic, honorable, beautiful, and aligned with God's truth. By nurturing new narratives that reflect God's values, we cultivate a mindset that honors Him and inspires others. You do not have to follow the world. Choose instead to dwell on positive, uplifting thoughts that align with God's Word, filling your mind with His goodness and truth.

 ## PERSONAL APPLICATION

What mental challenges are you facing today? What thoughts keep filling your mind?

Today, commit to nurturing new narratives in your mind. Intentionally focus on thoughts that are authentic, honorable, beautiful, and aligned with God's truth. Seek to cultivate a mindset that reflects His values and principles in all areas of your life and leadership. Choose to fasten your thoughts on the glorious works of God, praising Him always for His goodness and faithfulness. How are you fostering a healthy narrative among your friends and family? God's word is powerfully transformative.

REFLECTION

Reflect on the narratives that occupy your mind as a leader.

- ✔ What troubling thoughts are plaguing you?
- ✔ Consider the impact of your thoughts on your attitudes, perspectives, and interactions with others.
- ✔ Reflect on how aligning your thoughts with God's truth can influence your leadership style and relationships.
- ✔ How can you nurture new narratives that reflect authenticity, honor, beauty, and respect in your daily life?

AFFIRMATION

I am a leader who is committed to nurturing new narratives that align with God's truth. I choose to focus on thoughts that are authentic, honorable, beautiful, and aligned with His values. I can change my thoughts by focusing on His word. My mindset will reflect His goodness, mercy, and kindness, inspiring others and glorifying Him. I fasten my thoughts on the glorious works of God, praising Him always for His faithfulness and grace.

PRAYER

Dear Lord, as I surrender to you each day, guide me in nurturing new narratives that align with Your truth and values. Help me to focus on thoughts that are authentic, honorable, and beautiful, reflecting Your goodness and grace. May my mind be filled with thoughts that honor You and inspire others. Grant me the strength and wisdom to fasten my thoughts on Your glorious works, praising You always for Your faithfulness and love. Amen.

NETWORKING FOR KINGDOM IMPACT

> *Two people who work together are better than one person who works alone. They can help each other to work well. If one of them falls down, his friend can help him to get up. But it is terrible if you fall down when you are alone. There is nobody who can help you to stand up again.*
> Ecclesiastes 4:9-10 (Easy)

MEMORY SCRIPTURE

 DEVOTIONAL

As a leader, the power of networking and building relationships for Kingdom impact is significant. Therefore, relationships must be carefully chosen. Shared values exist within our circle of relationships. We don't lead alone; we lead with others. While we don't all share the exact same value system, the core foundation must honor God. That is a tie that brings us together. It is important to note that there may be unbelievers, who are still like-minded in terms of the goal, within your team. They may have important insights. Be careful to recognize their value as you work toward a common goal. Ecclesiastes 4:9-10 emphasizes the value of collaboration and partnership in achieving goals. Just as working with a friend provides support and encouragement, connecting with others in the Kingdom of God can amplify your impact and effectiveness. Embrace the idea of networking for Kingdom purposes, knowing that together you can make a greater difference in the lives of others.

 PERSONAL APPLICATION

Today, commit to networking for Kingdom impact.

Seek opportunities to connect with fellow believers, mentors, and like-minded individuals to collaborate on projects that advance God's Kingdom. Prioritize building relationships that support, encourage, and empower all of you. Choose to work alongside others who share a passion for making a difference. Through your collective efforts, all of you bring glory to God.

 REFLECTION

Reflect on the importance of networking and collaboration.

- ✔ Consider the impact of working together with others who share your Kingdom goals and values.
- ✔ Reflect on how building relationships can provide support, encouragement, and accountability in your leadership journey. How can you actively engage in networking for Kingdom impact to make a difference in the lives of those around you?
- ✔ Consider those within your sphere of networking and collaboration who are outside God's kingdom.
- ✔ Endeavor to allow them to see Christ at work within you.

 AFFIRMATION

I am a leader committed to networking for Kingdom impact. I will not isolate myself from others. Instead, I will embrace the value of collaboration and partnership in advancing God's Kingdom. I seek to build relationships that support, encourage, and empower me in my leadership journey. I seek to empower fellow believers, as well as those who may not be believers but who share a common goal with me. I strive to make a greater difference and bring glory to God through our collective efforts.

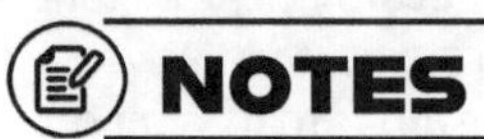 PRAYER

Dear Lord, guide me in networking for Kingdom impact as a leader. Help me to build relationships that support, encourage, and empower me and my team. Lead me to connect with like-minded individuals who share a passion for advancing Your Kingdom. May our collaborative efforts bring glory to Your name and make a lasting impact in the lives of others. Amen.

NOTES

NURTURING GOD'S GIFTS

> *Every believer has received grace gifts, so use them to serve one another as faithful stewards of the many-colored tapestry of God's grace. For example, if you have a speaking gift, speak as though God were speaking his words through you. If you have the gift of serving, do it passionately with the strength God gives you, so that in everything God alone will be glorified through Jesus Christ. For to him belong the power and the glory forever throughout all ages! Amen. 1 Peter 4:10-11 (TPT)*

MEMORY SCRIPTURE

 DEVOTIONAL

It is essential to recognize and nurture the gifts that God has entrusted to you. In 1 Peter 4:10-11, we are reminded that each of us has received gifts from God that we must use to serve others. So many individuals use their gifts for self-glorification rather than the exaltation of God's kingdom. Our gifts are God's ability working within us to bring glory to His name and to make Him known. It is important to understand what gifts we have been given and how and where we are to use them. Whether it is the gift of speaking, serving, leading, or any other talent, we are called to steward these gifts well for the glory of God. Embrace the responsibility of nurturing God's gifts with humility, diligence, and a heart of service, knowing that ultimately, all glory belongs to Him.

 PERSONAL APPLICATION

What gifts have you been given?

It is important to identify your gifts and talents so you can become proficient in using them. Everyone has been given at least one gift, so don't believe the lie the enemy tries to tell you that you don't have any gifts. Today, commit to nurturing the gifts that God has bestowed upon you. Seek to identify and develop these gifts to serve others with excellence and humility. Whether it is through speaking, serving, leading, teaching, nurturing, or any other talent, use these gifts to bring praise to God. Choose to serve with the strength and grace that God provides, acknowledging that all power and glory belong to Him forever.

🔍 REFLECTION

Reflect on the gifts that God has entrusted to you as a leader.

- ✔ How can you grow to understand more deeply and utilize the gifts you have been given?

- ✔ Consider how you have been using these gifts to serve others and bring glory to God.

- ✔ Reflect on the impact of nurturing and developing your gifts for Kingdom purposes.

- ✔ How can you further cultivate and utilize your gifts to make a meaningful impact in the lives of those you influence?

💬 AFFIRMATION

I am a leader committed to nurturing God's gifts for the service of others. I recognize the talents and abilities that God has bestowed upon me, and I choose to steward them well. With humility and diligence, I will develop and use these gifts to bring praise and glory to God. I serve with the strength and grace that He provides, knowing that all power and glory belong to Him forever.

🙏 PRAYER

Lord, thank you for entrusting me with gifts to serve others. Help me to nurture and develop these gifts with humility and diligence. Guide me in using these talents to bring praise and glory to Your name. May I serve with the strength and grace that You provide, acknowledging that all power and glory belong to You forever. Amen.

OVERCOMING SIN THROUGH GRACE

> *Remember this: sin will not conquer you, for God already has! You are not governed by law but governed by the reign of the grace of God.*
> Romans 6:14 (TPT)

MEMORY SCRIPTURE

DEVOTIONAL

The struggle with sin is a constant battle. Sin means to miss the mark. As you develop and grow in your faith, your spiritual capacity to resist the snares of the evil one will increase. God's grace is working within you, giving you power to overcome temptation. Grace is the manifestation of God's favor, kindness, and good will. The truth in Romans 6:14 reminds us that sin no longer has dominion over us because we are under the freedom of God's grace. Through His grace, we have the power to overcome sin and live a life that honors Him. Embrace the freedom that comes from God's grace, knowing that His love and forgiveness empower us to break free from the chains of sin and walk in righteousness. Receiving God's grace helps us to overcome bondage and the shame of living a life of sin.

 PERSONAL APPLICATION

Today, as you choose to overcome sin through the grace of God, you must embrace the freedom that comes from living under the grace of God, knowing that His love and forgiveness are greater than any sin.

This is not accomplished in our own human strength. It is not simply overcoming a bad habit or some other negative behavior. When we live according to His grace, He does a supernatural work in the desires of our hearts. We begin to seek to honor him rather than pleasing ourselves. Remember to seek His strength and guidance to resist temptation, confess your shortcomings, and strive to walk in righteousness. Surround yourself with strong believers who can encourage and pray for you when you are struggling. Commit to living a life that reflects the transformative power of God's grace in overcoming sin.

REFLECTION

Reflect on the power of God's grace in helping you to overcome sin. Consider the areas in your life where you may be struggling with temptation and in need of His grace.

- How can you rely on God's grace to overcome these challenges?
- What friend can you partner with in prayer to help you?
- Reflect on the freedom that comes from living under the grace of God and the victory you already have through His love and forgiveness.
- How can you rely on His grace to help you walk in righteousness?

AFFIRMATION

I am empowered to overcome sin through the grace of God. Sin is no longer my master, for I live under the freedom of God's grace. Sin no longer dominates me as I choose to walk in righteousness, relying on His strength and forgiveness to help me resist temptation and live a life that honors Him. Through His grace, I am set free from the chains of sin and empowered to live a life of victory.

PRAYER

Dear God, thank you for the freedom and grace that You have given me to overcome sin. Help me to rely on Your strength and forgiveness to resist temptation and walk in righteousness. Guide me in living a life that honors You and reflects the transformative power of Your grace. May Your love and grace empower me to overcome sin and live victoriously in Your presence. Amen.

OPTIMIZE OPPORTUNITIES

> *So be very careful how you live, not being like those with no understanding, but live honorably with true wisdom, for we are living in evil times. Take full advantage of every day as you spend your life for his purposes.*
> *Ephesians 5:15-16 (TPT)*

MEMORY SCRIPTURE

 DEVOTIONAL

It is crucial for leaders to optimize the opportunities that come their way. Procrastination is a deadly weapon used by the enemy to prevent us from optimizing opportunities. Ephesians 5:15-16 reminds us to live wisely and purposefully in a world filled with challenges. Each day presents new chances to make a positive impact, grow in wisdom, and live according to God's purposes. Embrace the call to be intentional and strategic in how you use your time and resources, seizing every opportunity to advance God's Kingdom and fulfill your God-given potential. Regardless of where you lead, whether it is in a great way or a small one, there are many opportunities each day to live for His purposes. Our lives are a gift from God and what we do with our life is a gift offered back to Him.

 PERSONAL APPLICATION

This doesn't mean that you are so driven that you violate the principles of rest and refreshment that govern our bodies. It also does not imply that you should forsake family and friends for the sake of your goals and ambitions. Live with wisdom and discernment, making intentional choices that align with God's purposes. Seize each day as a chance to make a difference, grow in your leadership skills, and contribute to the Kingdom of God. Choose to be proactive and strategic in how you use your time and talents, maximizing every opportunity to fulfill your calling and impact the lives of others.

 REFLECTION

Optimizing opportunities does not mean to live in imbalance or excess. Being a workaholic or any other type of excessive, addictive lifestyle is not what the Bible teaches. Consider how you can live wisely and purposefully, making the most of each day for God's purposes, and honoring the needs of your body and mind for care and rest.

- ✔ Reflect on the way you approach opportunities in your leadership journey.

- ✔ Do you have imbalances in your life and leadership?

- ✔ Does your daily schedule honor God?

- ✔ Reflect on the importance of being intentional and strategic in seizing opportunities to grow, serve, and make a positive impact. How did Jesus optimize opportunities to fulfill his mission?

- ✔ Remember how, after a day of preaching and healing, He often went alone into the desert to pray and refresh His soul in communion with His Heavenly Father. How can you stay whole and refreshed while you optimize the opportunities before you to advance God's Kingdom and fulfill your calling as a leader?

 AFFIRMATION

I am a leader committed to optimizing opportunities for God's purposes. I choose to live wisely and purposefully, making intentional choices that align with His will. Each day is a chance for me to grow, serve, and make a positive impact in the lives of others. I seize every opportunity to advance His Kingdom and fulfill my calling with passion and dedication. I resist the temptation to overwork, not get enough rest or sacrifice my time with God. I will live purposefully and in balance each day.

PRAYER

Dear God, guide me in optimizing opportunities for Your purposes. Grant me wisdom and discernment to make intentional choices that align with Your will. Help me to seize each day as a chance to grow, serve, and impact others for Your glory. Help me to live and serve in balance, focused on You each day. May I be proactive and strategic in using my time and talents to fulfill my calling and advance Your Kingdom. Amen.

NOTES

OVERCOMING OBSTACLES WITH FAITH

He told them, 'It was because of your lack of faith. I promise you, if you have faith inside of you no bigger than the size of a small mustard seed, you can say to this mountain, 'Move away from here and go over there,' and you will see it move! There is nothing you couldn't do!
Matthew 17:20 (TPT)

MEMORY SCRIPTURE

 DEVOTIONAL

Facing obstacles and challenges is inevitable. However, the key to overcoming these hurdles lies in having unwavering faith. It is during times of difficulties that our convictions are revealed. Faith is the key element in the life of believers, but faith is more than belief. Faith is intentional trust and confidence in God's power and ability to do what He has promised. In Matthew 17:20, Jesus reminds us of the power of faith, even as small as a mustard seed, to move mountains. Let this verse serve as a reminder that with faith you can conquer any obstacle that stands in your way. Trust in God's strength and believe that He can help you overcome every challenge you encounter.

 PERSONAL APPLICATION

Today, choose to overcome obstacles with faith.

Endeavor to cultivate a strong faith in God's power and promises, knowing that He is able to move mountains on your behalf. Face challenges with unwavering faith, trusting that God will provide the strength and wisdom needed to overcome them. Commit to relying on your mustard-seed-sized faith to conquer obstacles and achieve victory.

REFLECTION

Reflect on the obstacles you are currently facing in your leadership role.

- ✔ Consider how your faith has influenced your approach to challenges in the past.
- ✔ Reflect on moments when you have experienced God's faithfulness and provision in overcoming obstacles.
- ✔ How can you strengthen your faith and trust in God's power to help you conquer the mountains in your path?

AFFIRMATION

I am a leader who overcomes obstacles with unwavering faith. I walk by faith and not according to the limited vision of my eyes and mind. God has a plan for me, and He will help me face the obstacles that confront me as I journey toward His perfect plan. My trust in God's power and promises empowers me to face challenges with confidence and courage. With faith as small as a mustard seed, I believe that God can move the mountains in my life and leadership. I choose to rely on His strength and guidance to conquer every obstacle that comes my way.

PRAYER

Dear God, strengthen my faith as I face obstacles in my leadership journey. Help me to trust in Your power and promises, knowing that with faith, nothing is impossible. Grant me the courage and perseverance to overcome challenges with unwavering belief in Your ability to move mountains on my behalf. May my faith in You be a source of strength and victory in all circumstances. Amen.

NOTES

____

____

____

PURPOSEFUL PLANNING

> *Before you do anything, put your trust totally in God and not in yourself. Then every plan you make will succeed. Proverbs 16:3 (TPT)*

MEMORY SCRIPTURE

 DEVOTIONAL

Effective leadership requires purposeful planning. We take time to consider God's way for us to proceed. God's way is always the best way, and purposeful planning that includes prayer and meditation before God helps us to hear God's voice in our planning. The importance of purposeful planning cannot be overstated. In Proverbs 16:3, we are reminded to trust in God completely before making any plans, knowing that He is the ultimate source of wisdom and guidance. When we seek God's direction and align our plans with His will, we set ourselves up for success in every endeavor. Let this verse encourage you to prioritize purposeful planning that is rooted in God's leading and wisdom. Then allow God to do the rest!

 PERSONAL APPLICATION

Today, commit to purposeful planning and to trusting God completely before making any decisions or setting goals, seeking His guidance and direction in all your endeavors.

What plans are you considering? How will you include others in your planning? Prior to your meetings, take time before you start the day to offer up any decisions. Then let God direct the way you make your plans. Align your plans with His will and purpose, knowing that success comes from following His lead. Choose to prioritize purposeful planning that is centered on God's wisdom and not your own, and trust in His provision for every step of the journey.

🔍 REFLECTION

Reflect on your approach to planning and decision-making in your leadership role.

- ✔ Consider how often you seek God's guidance and trust in His direction before making plans.
- ✔ Reflect on the times when you have experienced success by aligning your plans with God's will.
- ✔ How can you deepen your trust in God and prioritize purposeful planning that honors His leading in your leadership journey?
- ✔ How can you avoid leaving God out of your decision-making process?
- ✔ Reflect on your short-term and long-term goals. How can you commit them to the Lord and seek His guidance in planning?

💬 AFFIRMATION

I am a leader who overcomes obstacles with unwavering faith. I walk by faith and not according to the limited vision of my eyes and mind. God has a plan for me, and He will help me face the obstacles that confront me as I journey toward His perfect plan. My trust in God's power and promises empowers me to face challenges with confidence and courage. With faith as small as a mustard seed, I believe that God can move the mountains in my life and leadership. I choose to rely on His strength and guidance to conquer every obstacle that comes my way.

🙏 PRAYER

Dear God, strengthen my faith as I face obstacles in my leadership journey. Help me to trust in Your power and promises, knowing that with faith, nothing is impossible. Grant me the courage and perseverance to overcome challenges with unwavering belief in

Your ability to move mountains on my behalf. May my faith in You be a source of strength and victory in all circumstances. Amen.

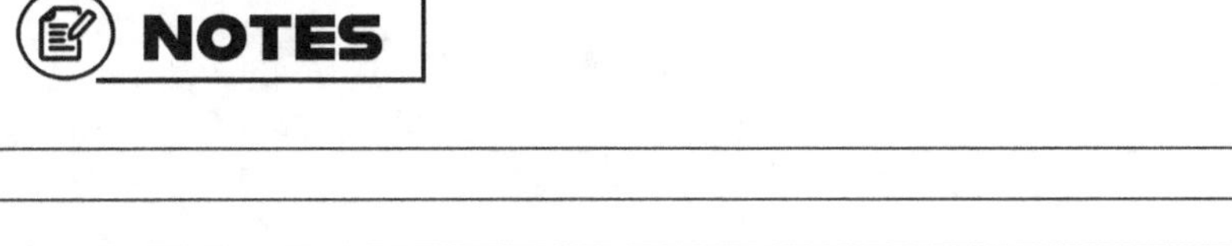

PRAYERFUL POSTURE

> **" Do not worry about anything. Instead, pray to God about everything. Ask him to help you with the things that you need. And thank him for his help. If you do that, God will give you peace in your minds. That peace is so great that nobody can completely understand it. You will not worry or be afraid, because you belong to Christ Jesus. Philippians 4:6-7 (Easy) "**

MEMORY SCRIPTURE

 DEVOTIONAL

Maintaining a prayerful posture is essential for navigating the challenges and opportunities that come your way. Early in our lives we learn to be independent and to do things for ourselves. This trait develops within us as we grow and mature. When we become a believer in Christ, we must learn to posture ourselves before him in prayer. Dependence on God develops as we posture ourselves in prayer. In Philippians 4:6-7, we are encouraged to be saturated in prayer, offering our requests to God with faith and gratitude. Prayer is an important discipline that must be cultivated in the life of every believer. By communicating with God and entrusting Him with every detail of our lives, we open ourselves up to His peace that surpasses understanding. Embrace a prayerful posture that aligns your heart and mind with God's will, knowing that He will make the answers known to you through the Holy Spirit.

 PERSONAL APPLICATION

Today, commit to embracing a prayerful posture.

Prioritize prayer throughout each day, offering your requests to God with faith and gratitude. Choose to share every detail of your life with Him, trusting that His peace will guard your heart and mind. Seek His guidance and wisdom through prayer, knowing that He will make the answers known to you in His perfect timing and through Jesus Christ.

REFLECTION

Reflect on the role of prayer in your leadership journey. Consider how often you turn to God in prayer and entrust Him with your concerns.

- ✔ Are you struggling with prayerlessness?
- ✔ What steps can you take to overcome this?
- ✔ What was the role of prayer in the life and ministry of Jesus?
- ✔ Identify a current concern and take a moment to bring it to God in prayer. How can cultivating a prayerful posture bring peace to your heart?
- ✔ Reflect on the peace that comes from communicating with God and seeking His guidance.
- ✔ How can you cultivate a more prayerful posture in your daily life as a leader and deepen your relationship with Him?

AFFIRMATION

I am a leader who embraces a prayerful posture in my life. I trust in God with every detail of my life, offering my requests with faith and gratitude. I refuse to allow myself to be more focused on my leadership responsibilities than on the One who has called me for His purposes. His peace guards my heart and mind, surpassing human understanding. Through prayer, I seek His guidance and wisdom, knowing that He will make the answers known to me through Jesus Christ in His perfect timing.

PRAYER

Dear God, guide me in embracing a prayerful posture as a leader. Teach me the power of prayer. Help me to be saturated in prayer, offering my requests to You with faith and gratitude. Guard my heart and mind with Your peace that surpasses understanding as I communicate with You and seek Your guidance. Make the answers known to me through Jesus Christ, and may my prayerful posture deepen my relationship with You and align my life with Your will. Amen.

QUALITIES OF A SERVANT LEADER

> *For even the Son of Man did not come expecting to be served by everyone, but to serve everyone, and to give his life as the ransom price for the salvation of many. Mark 10:45 (TPT)*

MEMORY SCRIPTURE

DEVOTIONAL

Embodying the qualities of a servant leader is essential if our hearts are set on following the example of Jesus Christ. Many worldly leaders allow themselves to function as taskmasters and not as servants. They call themselves leaders, but they are lost in pride, arrogance, and greed, not in true leadership. Seeking to be served and not serving others makes for an empty life and ends up being no use to anyone. In Mark 10:45, we are reminded that Jesus came not to be served, but to serve and give His life for others. A servant leader leads with humility, compassion, and a heart of service, prioritizing the needs of others above their own. Embrace the call to emulate Jesus' servant leadership, recognizing that true greatness is found in serving and sacrificing for the sake of others.

PERSONAL APPLICATION

Servant leadership lies beyond our titles and positions. Rather, it is an opportunity to model humility as you find ways to uplift those around you.

Commit today to embodying the qualities of a servant leader. Lead with humility, compassion, and a heart of service, following the example set by Jesus Christ. Choose to prioritize the needs of others above your own, seeking opportunities to serve, support, and uplift those around you. Endeavor to give of yourself selflessly and sacrificially, reflecting the true essence of servant leadership in all aspects of your life and leadership.

 REFLECTION

Reflect on the qualities of a servant leader as exemplified by Jesus Christ in Mark 10:45.

- ✔ Consider how you can cultivate humility, compassion, and a heart of service in your leadership style.
- ✔ Consider leaders who have inspired you through servant leadership. How can their example guide your own leadership journey?
- ✔ Reflect on the impact of serving others selflessly and sacrificially in your personal and professional relationships.
- ✔ How can you emulate Jesus' example of servant leadership in your daily interactions and decision-making as a leader?
- ✔ Identify someone around you to whom you can show a random act of kindness by affirming their contributions or assisting them in some way.

AFFIRMATION

I am a leader committed to embodying the qualities of a servant leader. I choose to lead with humility, compassion, and a heart of service, following the example of Jesus Christ. I prioritize the needs of others above my own, seeking opportunities to serve and uplift those around me. I will watch for opportunities to serve those around me. Through selflessness and sacrificial leadership, I reflect the true essence of service.

PRAYER

Dear Lord, guide me in embodying the qualities of a servant leader. Help me to lead with humility, compassion, and a heart of service, following the example set by Jesus Christ. Grant me the strength and wisdom to prioritize the needs of others above my own, seeking opportunities to serve and uplift those around me. May my leadership reflect the true essence of servant leadership and bring glory to Your name. Amen.

QUIET TIME WITH GOD

> *Surrender your anxiety! Be still and realize that I am God. I am God above all the nations, and I am exalted throughout the whole earth. Psalm 46:10 (TPT)*

MEMORY SCRIPTURE

 DEVOTIONAL

We live in a noisy world. Every day there are so many things clamoring for our attention. It can be overwhelming. Stress and anxiety are all too common among leaders. The inability to relax in stillness escapes them. Finding time for quiet reflection and communion with God is essential for spiritual growth and renewal. When we lack time for communion, our exhaustion can manifest itself in ill-temper or impatience. These traits don't honor either our leadership or God. In Psalm 46:10, we are reminded to surrender our anxieties, be silent, and cease striving, allowing God to reveal His presence and power in our lives. Through quiet time with God, we can experience His peace, wisdom, and guidance, acknowledging His sovereignty and exalting Him above all else. Discipline yourself to embrace the stillness and seek God's presence in moments of quiet reflection and prayer.

 PERSONAL APPLICATION

Today, commit to prioritizing quiet time with God.

What things are creating anxiety in you? Surrender any anxieties, be silent, and cease striving, allowing God to speak to your heart and reveal His presence. Choose to seek His peace, wisdom, and guidance in moments of stillness, acknowledging His sovereignty over all things. Make space in your day for quiet reflection and communion with God, knowing that in His presence you find renewal and strength.

 REFLECTION

Reflect on the importance of quiet time with God.

- ✔ Are you experiencing stress and anxiety?

- ✔ Do you struggle to sleep at night, tossing and turning rather than having a peaceful night's rest?

- ✔ Consider how moments of stillness and silence can deepen your relationship with God and provide clarity and direction. Reflect on the significance of surrendering anxieties and striving, allowing God to reveal His presence and power in your life.

- ✔ Dedicate intentional time today to be still in God's presence. How can quiet time with Him deepen your understanding of His nature?

- ✔ Recall moments of stillness you've spent in God's presence. How have they impacted your spiritual journey?

AFFIRMATION

I am a leader who prioritizes quiet time with God for spiritual growth and renewal. I surrender my anxieties, become silent, and cease striving, allowing Him to reveal His presence and power in my life. In moments of stillness, I seek His peace, wisdom, and guidance, acknowledging His sovereignty over all things. Through quiet reflection and communion with God, I find renewal, strength, and direction. I will lie down in His peace and rest well at night because His peace surrounds me.

PRAYER

Dear God, guide me in prioritizing quiet time with You. Help me to surrender my anxieties, become silent, and cease striving, allowing Your presence to bring peace and clarity to my heart. Grant me wisdom and guidance as I seek Your direction in moments of stillness and reflection. May my quiet time with You be a source of renewal and strength for my leadership journey, exalting Your name above all else. Amen.

ADDITIONAL NOTES

ADDITIONAL NOTES

RESILIENCE IN ADVERSITY

> *My fellow believers, when it seems as though you are facing nothing but difficulties, see it as an invaluable opportunity to experience the greatest joy that you can! For you know that when your faith is tested, it stirs up power within you to endure all things. And then as your endurance grows even stronger it will release perfection into every part of your being until there is nothing missing and nothing lacking.*
> James 1:2-4 (TPT)

MEMORY SCRIPTURE

DEVOTIONAL

Facing challenges and adversity is an inevitable part of your leadership journey. All the components of leadership-team building, vision casting, supporting others in their own leadership journeys and even finding your own voice as a leader-are challenging. There are times when your well-meant efforts are misunderstood. Maybe you have even been blamed for something that was not of your doing. Adversity is simply part of life. What matters is how we process it. In James 1:2-4, we are reminded that difficulties can be opportunities for growth and resilience. When our faith is tested, it stirs up a power within us to endure with patience and discover unexpected strength. Especially when someone hurts us or deals with us unfairly, we must never retaliate in kind. That doesn't mean that we can't stand up for ourselves, but we must do it in ways that don't set more hurt and unfairness loose in the world. Embrace adversity as a chance to develop resilience, strength, insight, and endurance, knowing that it will lead to a more perfect and complete version of yourself. Let challenges be stepping stones to greater joy and maturity in your leadership.

PERSONAL APPLICATION

Adversity is something that you will face throughout your life. It seems overwhelming.

The taunt of the enemy will attempt to discourage you and influence you to believe that life would be easier if you were not a follower of Jesus. Your faith will be tested. In these moments, recognize that the enemy of your soul can only have the victory if you yield to it. By the power of Jesus Christ, you can win. Like a tree buffeted by the wind, but not broken, commit to cultivating resilience. See challenges as opportunities to grow in faith, strength, and endurance. When difficulties arise, approach them with a mindset of perseverance and trust in God's power to sustain you. Choose to view adversity as a pathway to greater joy and maturity, knowing that through endurance, you will be perfected and lack nothing.

REFLECTION

Recall a time when God's faithfulness sustained you through adversity.

- ✔ How can that experience encourage you to persevere in the face of challenges?

- ✔ Examine the way you respond to challenges and adversity. What areas of your life is the enemy targeting?

- ✔ Where is it easiest for you to feel discouraged?

- ✔ Remember the forty days Jesus spent alone in the wilderness before He began His mission, and how the enemy tempted him there. How did Jesus respond to that testing? He knew that He had to stand up to the enemy and endure the testing faithfully before He could set out on His mission.

- ✔ Consider your own wilderness times, and how difficulties have shaped your faith, strength, and resilience.

- ✔ Reflect on the power that is stirred within you when your faith is tested and how endurance leads to growth and maturity.

- ✔ How can you embrace adversity as an opportunity to develop resilience and trust in God's provision in every situation?

AFFIRMATION

I am a leader committed to cultivating resilience in the face of adversity. I see challenges as opportunities for growth and strength. When my faith is tested, I trust in God's power to sustain me and help me to endure. I will follow the example of Jesus and submit to God's power at work within me. Adversity is a pathway to greater joy and maturity in my leadership journey, and through perseverance, I am perfected and lack nothing.

PRAYER

Dear God, grant me the strength and resilience to face challenges and adversity with faith and endurance. Help me to see difficulties as opportunities for growth and maturity in my leadership journey. Help me to follow the example set by Jesus and stand strong in these challenging times. Stir up the power within me to persevere and trust in Your provision through every trial. May adversity lead me to greater joy and completeness in my life, knowing that in You, I lack nothing. Amen.

NOTES

RENEWED STRENGTH

> *But people who wait for the Lord to help them will receive new strength. They will rise up high, as if they have the wings of eagles. They will run and they will not become tired. They will walk and they will not become weak.*
> *Isaiah 40:31 (Easy)*

MEMORY SCRIPTURE

 DEVOTIONAL

Leadership is demanding. Whether you are a CEO or janitor, you are faced daily with the challenges that come with leadership. Perhaps you are a stay-at-home parent faced with leading your children so that they stay safe, whole, and healthy. Or you are caring for a mother or father or spouse who can no longer care for themselves. Wherever you are, you are carrying a heavy load. But you are still a leader, even when depression and exhaustion drain your strength, and you feel that you have no more to give. Perhaps as you are reading this, you may be feeling weary and depleted, facing challenges that drain your energy and resolve. Remember, there is a reserve of strength available far beyond your own. In Isaiah 40:31, we are reminded that those who wait for God's grace will experience divine strength. Just as eagles soar effortlessly on the wind, we are called to rise above our circumstances and find renewed strength in God. It's not weakness to ask God for it. If you do, surprising things will happen, like lights suddenly coming on in a dark room or waking up to sunlight after a night of storm. Embrace the promise of divine strength that enables you to run your race without growing weary and walk through life without giving up.

 PERSONAL APPLICATION

Today, don't give up.

Ask God for courage to commit to waiting on His grace for renewed strength. Seek His presence and wait expectantly for His divine provision. When you feel weary or discouraged, the Holy Spirit can help you rise above your circumstances and find renewed energy to run your race with perseverance. Even when you are too tired to think and struggle to find the words to pray, choose to trust in God's power to sustain you in every situation.

REFLECTION

Consider moments when you have felt weary and depleted, overwhelmed, and discouraged.

- ✔ Identify an area in your life where you need to have your strength renewed. Where have you given up thinking that your situation will not get better? Tired as you are, can you still turn to the Lord and say, "I can't anymore, but You can. Please help!"

- ✔ Reflect on how waiting on God's grace and seeking His strength has renewed your energy and resolve.

- ✔ Remember His promise of divine strength that enables you to soar above challenges and run your race with endurance.

- ✔ How can you cultivate a spirit of waiting on God's grace for renewed strength in your daily life as a leader?

AFFIRMATION

I will not give up, but I will wait on God's grace for renewed strength. In His presence, I find divine energy to overcome challenges and run my race with perseverance. Like an eagle soaring on the wind, I rise above weariness and walk through life with resilience and determination. In God's strength, I find renewal and endurance to fulfill my purpose and calling.

PRAYER

Dear God, grant me the grace to always wait on You for renewed strength. Give me Your courage that I might overcome discouragement. Fill me with Your divine energy to overcome challenges and run my race with perseverance. Help me to soar above weariness and discouragement and walk through life with resilience and determination. May Your strength sustain me in every situation, enabling me to fulfill my purpose and calling with renewed vigor and endurance. Amen.

NOTES

STEWARDSHIP OF TALENTS

> *God has helped each of you in a certain way. Think carefully about how to use that gift from God well. Remember that God has given many different gifts to his people so that they can help each other. 1 Peter 4:10 (TPT)*

MEMORY SCRIPTURE

DEVOTIONAL

It is essential to recognize the talents and gifts that God has entrusted to you and use them to serve others. The gifts you have been given are designed to increase your influence so that others will see Christ at work within you and desire fellowship with Him. These are not our gifts to use however we please. Rather, our gifts are designed to bring glory to God. In 1 Peter 4:10, we are reminded that each of us has received a gift to use in serving others, and we are called to be good stewards of these gifts of grace. Your talents are not meant to be hidden or wasted but are to be used to make a positive impact and serve those around you. Don't be afraid of using them! Allow your gifts to shine for God's glory. Embrace the responsibility of stewarding your talents well and dedicate them to the glory of God.

PERSONAL APPLICATION

Today, commit to stewarding your talents for the service of others, for when you serve others, you serve God.

What gifts has God given you and how are you using them? Identify and develop your God-given gifts and commit to using them to make a positive impact and serve those around you. Choose to be a good steward of God's various gifts of grace, recognizing the responsibility and privilege that comes with using your talents for

His purposes. Seek opportunities to serve others and bring glory to God through the unique gifts He has bestowed upon you.

🔍 REFLECTION

Reflect on the talents and gifts that God has entrusted to you.

- ✔ Consider how you have been using these gifts to serve others and make a positive impact. Have you withdrawn in fear of what others might say?
- ✔ Do you feel self-conscious and intimidated when your gifts are the solution and should be shared with others?
- ✔ How can stewarding your gifts be a form of worship?
- ✔ Reflect on the responsibility of stewarding your talents well and the privilege of being entrusted with God's gifts of grace.
- ✔ How can you further develop and utilize your talents to serve others and bring glory to God?

AFFIRMATION

: I am committed to stewarding my talents for the service of others. I recognize the gifts that God has given me and the responsibility to use them for His glory. I choose to be a good steward of God's various gifts of grace, seeking opportunities to serve and make a positive impact with the talents He has entrusted to me. Through the use of my gifts, I bring honor and glory to God in all that I do.

🙏 PRAYER

Dear God, thank you for the gifts and talents that You have bestowed upon me. Help me to steward these gifts well and use them to serve others and bring glory to Your name. Guide me in identifying and developing the talents You have given me, so that I may make a positive impact and fulfill Your purposes. Help me to be bold in using my gifts for your glory. May I be a good servant of Your gifts of grace and seek opportunities to serve others with humility and love. Amen.

TIME MANAGEMENT FOR KINGDOM BUILDING

> *So be very careful how you live, not being like those with no understanding, but live honorably with true wisdom, for we are living in evil times. Take full advantage of every day as you spend your life for his purposes.*
> Ephesians 5:15-16 (TPT)

MEMORY SCRIPTURE

 DEVOTIONAL

Effective time management is crucial for building God's Kingdom and fulfilling His purposes. This includes making time for your spiritual growth and development. We only need to look at our families, communities, and nations to see the depravity of humanity. Violence, addictions, divorce, and other societal ills are everywhere. We are witnessing moral failure among spiritual leaders. Much of this stems from the lack of understanding of how to live honorably, with true wisdom in the midst of evil. In Ephesians 5:15-16, we are reminded to live with wisdom and honor, making the most of every day in a world filled with distractions and challenges. Time is a precious resource that should be used wisely for the advancement of God's Kingdom. As believers, our lives are meant to reflect God at work within us. Embrace the call to manage your time intentionally, prioritizing activities that align with His purposes and bring honor to His name.

 PERSONAL APPLICATION

Commit to seeking wisdom and understanding in the way you live, making honorable choices that reflect true wisdom.

Effective time management is critical for the building of God's Kingdom. Time management includes making time for spiritual development. We are more than our professions. True wisdom is understanding the principle of 'Christ first' and allowing His power to flow through us. When we cultivate a daily practice of spending time reading the word of God, along with prayer and worship, we access wisdom and understanding that helps us navigate our lives. Choose to take full advantage of every day, using your time purposefully for God's purposes. You are helping to build God's kingdom here on Earth. Prioritize activities that align with God's Kingdom and bring glory to His name, managing your time in a way that reflects your commitment to His Kingdom.

🔍 REFLECTION

Reflect on the importance of living with wisdom and true understanding in a world filled with distractions.

- ✔ Consider the activities and priorities that occupy your days and whether they align with God's purposes. How do you currently manage your time?

- ✔ How do you schedule time for spiritual growth and development?

- ✔ Remember you are more than money and promotion. You were created for the purposes of God. In your leadership role, how can you take full advantage of every day and manage your time effectively for the building of God's Kingdom?

- ✔ Are there areas where you can improve in being more intentional and strategic with your time? Is entertainment filling up your time when you are not working?

- ✔ Are there opportunities for growth and leadership development that you may be missing because of distractions or lack of focus?

💬 AFFIRMATION

I am committed to managing my time effectively for the building of God's Kingdom. I choose to live with wisdom and honor, making purposeful choices that align with His purposes. I take full advantage of every day, using my time intentionally to bring glory to God and advance His Kingdom. Managing my time includes making time for my spiritual growth and development. Through effective time management, I fulfill my calling to serve and build for His glory.

PRAYER

Dear God, guide me in managing my time effectively for the building of Your Kingdom. Grant me wisdom and understanding to make honorable choices that reflect Your purposes. Help me to take full advantage of every day, using my time purposefully for Your glory. May my time management reflect my commitment to serving and building for Your Kingdom, bringing honor and praise to Your name. Amen.

NOTES

TRUSTING GOD'S TIMING

> *There is a right time for everything. Everything that we do on earth has a proper time.*
> *Ecclesiastes 3:1 (Easy)*

MEMORY SCRIPTURE

 DEVOTIONAL

We live in a fast-paced society. Instant gratification has become the norm. We are no longer content to wait, we want everything now. This way of thinking and being causes us to move outside of God's timing. God has planned your life, and within His plan is time. We must learn to wait for His plan and time. He cultivates patience in us so that we are able to wait more peacefully. It can be challenging to wait for God's timing in the midst of a fast-paced world that demands immediate results. Ecclesiastes 3:1 reminds us that there is a time for everything, and each season in life has its purpose and significance. Trusting God's timing requires patience, faith, and surrender to His perfect plans. Embrace the assurance that God orchestrates the seasons of your life, and His timing is always perfect. Allow yourself to rest in His sovereignty and trust in His faithfulness.

 PERSONAL APPLICATION

What are you waiting for? Like children before Christmas who can't wait to open their new gifts, we as adults often find waiting difficult. We want to see everything God promised us right now.

Perhaps you are just beginning your career, and you have pinned all your hopes and dreams upon it. You have worked toward it for so long, and now you have to accept that it takes time to build the amazing career you have been dreaming about and God has planned.

It won't happen overnight. Today, though you may not understand all that it means, you must commit to trusting God's timing in every aspect of your life. Surrender your desires for immediate results and embrace the seasons that God has ordained for you. Choose to have patience and faith in His perfect plans, knowing that His timing is always right. Intentionally seek to align your actions and decisions with His timing, trusting that He will fulfill His purposes in your life at the appointed time.

 REFLECTION

Recall times when God's timing was evident in your life.

- ✔ When have you had an experience when you didn't wait for God's timing? What was the result?

- ✔ How can those experiences deepen your trust in His plan?

- ✔ As a leader, reflect on the concept of trusting God's timing. Consider areas in your life where you may be struggling to wait for His perfect timing. What are some simple strategies that can help you wait patiently?

- ✔ Reflect on the truth that each season has its purpose and significance in God's plan for your life. How can you cultivate a spirit of patience and faith in His timing, trusting that He is working all things together for your good?

AFFIRMATION

I am a leader who trusts in God's timing for every season of my life. I surrender my desires for immediate results and embrace His perfect plans. I commit to not leaning on my own understanding and doing things my own way. With patience and faith, I align my actions with His timing, knowing that He orchestrates every season for my good. I trust in His sovereignty and rest in the assurance that His timing is always perfect.

 PRAYER

Lord Jesus, grant me the strength and faith to trust in Your timing. Help me to surrender my desires for immediate results and embrace the seasons that You have ordained for me. Give me patience and wisdom to align my actions with Your perfect plans, knowing that Your timing is always right. I endeavor to rest in Your sovereignty and trust in Your faithfulness, believing that You are working all things together for my good. Amen.

NOTES

UNDERSTANDING GOD'S WORD

> *Break open your Word within me until revelation-light shines out! Those with open hearts are given insight into your plans.*
> Psalm 119:130 (TPT)

MEMORY SCRIPTURE

 DEVOTIONAL

God's word is vital for our spiritual growth and development. The more we read and meditate on God's word, the more we grow in understanding. Leaders should seek to understand and apply God's Word as an essential component of spiritual growth and wisdom. In Psalm 119:130, we are reminded that understanding God's Word illuminates our minds and brings clarity to our thoughts. The Scriptures are a source of light that guides us in our decision-making, leadership, and daily life. Embrace the transformative power of God's Word to bring wisdom, insight, and understanding to your journey as a leader.

 PERSONAL APPLICATION

Thanks to the presence of media everywhere, many people no longer or seldom read. The normalizing of social media has produced a generation of leaders who opt for watching something on a screen rather than reading their Bible.

The habit of reading and re-reading a beloved text to discern its deepest meaning is being lost. Resist the tendency to avoid reading God's word. Commit to seeking understanding in God's Word. This begins with reading His word, and then reading it over and over again until your soul discovers its significance. Seek to immerse yourself in Scripture, allowing its truths to illuminate your mind and guide your thoughts. Choose to prioritize studying and applying God's Word in your life and leadership, seeking wisdom and insight for every decision and action. Rely on the light of His Word to bring clarity and understanding to your path as you lead others with grace and wisdom.

 ## REFLECTION

Reflect on the importance of understanding God's Word in your personal life and leadership role.

- ✔ How can you deepen your understanding of God's Word and apply its truths to your leadership journey?

- ✔ Spend time with God's Word today and return to it tomorrow. How can the understanding of His Word bring light to your current circumstances?

- ✔ Consider how Scripture has illuminated your mind and guided your thoughts in the past.

- ✔ Reflect on the transformative power of God's Word to bring wisdom and insight to your decision-making and actions as a leader.

 ## AFFIRMATION

I will seek understanding in God's Word for wisdom and guidance. The Scriptures bring light to my mind and clarity to my thoughts, illuminating my path as I lead others. I prioritize studying and applying God's Word in my life and leadership, seeking wisdom and insight for every decision. Through the transformative power of His Word, I lead with grace, wisdom, and understanding.

 ## PRAYER

Dear God, as I continue my leadership journey, grant me the desire to seek understanding in Your Word. Illuminate my mind with the truths of Scripture and guide my thoughts in wisdom and insight. Help me to prioritize studying and applying Your Word, seeking

Your guidance for every decision and action I make. May Your Word bring light and clarity to my path, as I lead others with grace, wisdom, and understanding. Amen.

NOTES

Unity in Diversity

> **Be faithful to guard the sweet harmony of the Holy Spirit among you in the bonds of peace.**
> **Ephesians 4:3 (TPT)**

MEMORY SCRIPTURE

 DEVOTIONAL

Some of us are tall, some of us are short, and some of us are in the middle. Some are male, others are female. Our physical features, ethnicities and social and economic backgrounds are all different. But though those differences may count in the eyes of the world, they are only superficial. In God's eyes, while each of us is unique and has been created in His image and likeness, we are all His people. We have been given gifts and talents not only to accomplish God's purpose for our own lives but also so that we can work together effectively for the sake of all our lives. Without unity in diversity, we can find ourselves focused on differences and allow those differences to divide us. This is not God's plan, and it is not effective for leaders. Embracing unity in diversity is key to fostering a harmonious and inclusive environment that reflects God's love for us all. Leaders must endeavor to create cultures of unity. In Ephesians 4:3, we are reminded to guard the sweet harmony of the Holy Spirit among us, binding us together in peace. Unity in diversity celebrates the unique gifts, perspectives, and backgrounds that each individual brings, creating a rich tapestry of collaboration and understanding. Embrace the call to cultivate unity, respect, and love as you lead, honoring the diversity that strengthens and enriches your family, friends, and co-workers.

PERSONAL APPLICATION

Commit to fostering unity in diversity.

Honoring the diversity around you creates space for the unique gifts and talents of everyone. Guard the harmony of the Holy Spirit among those you lead, promoting peace and understanding in all interactions. Choose to celebrate the diverse gifts, perspectives, and backgrounds of those around you, recognizing the value each individual brings to the table. As you strive to create an inclusive and welcoming environment that honors and respects the uniqueness of every person within your circle of influence, you will foster unity and collaboration in all that you do.

REFLECTION

Consider how diversity strengthens and enriches those within your sphere of influence.

- ✔ How are you different from those on your team?
- ✔ How are their gifts different from yours?
- ✔ Reflect on the significance of guarding the harmony of the Holy Spirit and promoting peace and understanding in all your interactions.
- ✔ How can you actively foster unity, respect, and love toward your family, friends, and co-workers, embracing and celebrating the unique contributions that each individual brings to the table?

AFFIRMATION

I am a leader committed to fostering unity in diversity within my team. I honor and celebrate the unique gifts, perspectives, and backgrounds of each individual, recognizing the value they bring. I will guard the harmony of the Holy Spirit among us, promoting peace and understanding in all interactions. Through unity in diversity, we create a culture of inclusion, respect, and collaboration that strengthens and enriches our team.

 PRAYER

Dear God, guide me in fostering unity and peace. Within our unique differences and distinctions, we honor you through respect for each other. Help me to guard the sweet harmony of the Holy Spirit among those I influence, promoting peace and understanding in all interactions. Grant me the wisdom and humility to honor and celebrate the difference of gifts and perspectives within my team. May Your love and grace bind us together in unity, creating a culture of inclusion, respect, and collaboration that glorifies Your name. Amen.

NOTES

VICTORIOUS LIVING

> *But we thank God for giving us the victory as conquerors through our Lord Jesus, the Anointed One. 1 Corinthians 15:57 (TPT)*

MEMORY SCRIPTURE

 DEVOTIONAL

Being a leader doesn't mean you won't make mistakes. You can't be a real leader without making yourself vulnerable and being vulnerable means making mistakes. God's grace and forgiveness keeps us from becoming paralyzed in the moment of a mistake. Even though we often can't help making mistakes because we are human, we can ask for forgiveness and still embrace a mindset of victorious living. It is essential for navigating the challenges and triumphs of our leadership journey. Mistakes are learning opportunities, not defining moments. In 1 Corinthians 15:57, we are reminded that through our Lord Jesus, we have been given the victory as conquerors. Victorious living is not about the absence of challenges but about overcoming them with faith, strength, and perseverance. Embrace the assurance that in Christ, you are equipped to triumph over obstacles and live victoriously in His power.

 PERSONAL APPLICATION

Victorious living is not the result of self-effort but the result of yielding our lives to the Lord.

Be willing to submit your struggles to the Lord as you commit to embracing a mindset of victorious living. Recognize victories no matter how small and thank God for them. Remember that through Jesus Christ you are empowered to conquer challenges and obstacles. Choose to approach each day with faith, strength, and perseverance, knowing that you are equipped to overcome any difficulties that come your way. Commit to walking in the confidence of Christ's victory, living triumphantly in His power and grace.

 REFLECTION

Reflect on what it means to live victoriously as a leader.

- ✔ Identify an area where you feel defeated. How can you claim the victory that Christ has already secured for you?
- ✔ What did Jesus do to secure victory when He was on Earth?
- ✔ Consider the challenges and obstacles you have faced and how God has given you the victory through Jesus Christ.
- ✔ Reflect on the assurance of triumphing over difficulties with faith, strength, and perseverance.
- ✔ How can you cultivate a mindset of victorious living, leaning on Christ's power and grace to overcome obstacles and achieve success?

AFFIRMATION

I am a leader who embraces a mindset of victorious living. Through Jesus Christ, I have been given the victory as a conqueror over challenges and obstacles. I approach each day with faith, strength, and perseverance, knowing that I am equipped to overcome any difficulties. In Christ, I walk in confidence and triumph, living victoriously in His power and grace.

PRAYER

Dear God, thank you for giving me the victory as a conqueror through Jesus Christ. Empower me to embrace a mindset of victorious living, overcoming challenges with faith, strength, and perseverance. Help me to walk in the confidence of Your victory, living triumphantly in Your power and grace. May Your presence and guidance lead me to achieve success and fulfill Your purposes as I lead others. Amen.

WORSHIPFUL LIVING

With all my heart and passion I will thank you, my God! I will give glory to your name, always and forever! Psalm 86:12 (TPT)

MEMORY SCRIPTURE

 DEVOTIONAL

Committing to a lifestyle of worshipful living is a powerful way to honor and glorify God in all aspects of your life. In Psalm 86:12, we are reminded of the importance of thankfulness. Some believers find it difficult to worship God with hearts and voices. They draw back from physical expressions of praise and thanksgiving. They need to remember that lifting up our voices in praise and thanksgiving and our hands in adoration is an outpouring of our passion for God. Not only are the Psalms of David songs that were sung to the Lord, but King David even danced before the Ark of the Lord. We are admonished to love God with all our heart's passion, our minds, and our strength, giving glory to His name always and forever. That includes our voices and our bodies. Worshipful living involves recognizing God's presence in every moment, offering gratitude, praise, and adoration for His goodness and faithfulness. Embrace the joy of living a life that exalts God's name and magnifies His greatness through worship with all our being.

 PERSONAL APPLICATION

Today, commit to living a lifestyle of worship.

With all your heart and passion, thank God and give glory to His name in every aspect of your life. Choose to cultivate a heart of gratitude, praise, and adoration, recognizing God's presence and faithfulness in all circumstances. Find times throughout your day to audibly honor God. Seek to honor and magnify His greatness through worshipful living, exalting His name always and forever. Find moments throughout the day to honor God in singing, clapping, and thanksgiving.

 REFLECTION

Reflect on what it means to live a lifestyle of worship as a leader.

- ✔ Consider the ways in which you can express gratitude, praise, and adoration to God in your daily life. Don't be shy about giving audible praise to God.

- ✔ Reflect on the joy and fulfillment that come from honoring God and magnifying His greatness through worshipful living.

- ✔ How can you integrate worship into your leadership journey, exalting His name in all that you do?

AFFIRMATION

I am committed to living a lifestyle of worship. I will sing to the Lord a new song. With all my heart and passion, I thank God and give glory to His name always and forever. I cultivate a heart of gratitude, praise, and adoration, honoring God's presence and faithfulness in every moment. Through worshipful living, I magnify His greatness and exalt His name in all aspects of my life.

PRAYER

Dear God, I thank you with all my heart and passion for your goodness and faithfulness toward me. Help me to cultivate a lifestyle of worship as a leader, offering gratitude, praise, and adoration to your name always and forever. May my life reflect your greatness, exalting your name in all that I do. Guide me in living a life that honors and glorifies you through worshipful living. Amen.

WITNESSING WITH WISDOM

Walk in the wisdom of God as you live before the unbelievers and make it your duty to make him known. Let every word you speak be drenched with grace and tempered with truth and clarity. For then you will be prepared to give a respectful answer to anyone who asks about your faith. Colossians 4:5-6 (TPT)

MEMORY SCRIPTURE

 DEVOTIONAL

Sharing your faith and witnessing to others requires wisdom, grace, and clarity. As influencers, our words and actions are ways in which we model the ways in which believers live and lead. The message of faith in Christ must be clear and consistent but not overbearing. Using our position of leadership to engage in forceful, intimidating witnessing does not honor God. In Colossians 4:5-6, we are encouraged to walk in the wisdom of God as we interact with unbelievers, making it our duty to make Him known in the way we live our lives. Keep yourself free of negativity and judgmentalism. It is essential to let every word you speak be filled with grace and truth, reflecting the love of Christ in your interactions. Through wisdom, grace, and clarity, you can effectively share your faith and be prepared to give a respectful answer to those who inquire about your beliefs.

 PERSONAL APPLICATION

Today, commit to witnessing with wisdom.

Purpose to walk in the wisdom of God as you interact with others, sharing His love and truth. Choose to speak words drenched with grace and tempered with truth and clarity, reflecting the love of Christ in all your interactions. Avoid berating others concerning their beliefs and convictions. Rather, choose to be a model of Christ's love for humanity. Be prepared to give a respectful answer to anyone who asks about your faith, sharing the hope and joy that you have in Christ with wisdom and grace.

 REFLECTION

Reflect on the importance of witnessing with wisdom.

- ✔ Consider how you can effectively share your faith and make God known to those around you.
- ✔ Reflect on the significance of letting your words be filled with grace and truth, reflecting the love of Christ.
- ✔ How can you cultivate a spirit of wisdom, grace, and clarity in your witness, preparing to share the hope of Christ with others?

 AFFIRMATION

I am committed to witnessing with wisdom, grace, and clarity. I walk in the wisdom of God as I interact with others, making it my duty to share His love and truth. Every word I speak is drenched with grace and tempered with truth, reflecting the love of Christ in all my interactions. I am prepared to give a respectful answer to anyone who asks about my faith, sharing the hope and joy I have in Christ with wisdom and grace.

PRAYER

Lord Jesus, grant me wisdom, grace, and clarity as I witness to others. Help me to make You known in all that I do and say, reflecting Your love and truth to those around me. May every word I speak be filled with grace and tempered with truth, reflecting the love of Christ in all interactions. Prepare me to give a respectful answer to anyone who asks about my faith, sharing the hope and joy I have in You with wisdom and grace. Amen.

ADDITIONAL NOTES

ADDITIONAL NOTES

eXAMINING YOUR HEART

> **God, I invite your searching gaze into my heart. Examine me through and through; find out everything that may be hidden within me. Put me to the test and sift through all my anxious cares. See if there is any path of pain I'm walking on, and lead me back to your glorious, everlasting way—the path that brings me back to you. Psalm 139:23-24 (TPT)**

MEMORY SCRIPTURE

DEVOTIONAL

Leaders are not exempt from offences, anger, worry, and other negative emotions. Relationship issues, problems with co-workers, or even the loss of a job can be the catalyst for toxic emotions. Anger, bitterness, and resentment can enter an unguarded heart in these moments. It is essential to examine your heart daily, allowing God to search the depths of your inner being. In today's scripture, the psalmist invites God to scrutinize and reveal any hidden or anxious thoughts within him. Through this process of examination, we open ourselves up to God's correction, guidance, and transformation. Embrace the opportunity to allow God to reveal areas in your heart that need healing, restoration, or redirection, leading you back to His glorious and everlasting ways.

PERSONAL APPLICATION

Resentment, bitterness, and other toxic emotions can affect both your leadership and your witness.

Oftentimes we say we are over something, but we are not. The little foxes of bitterness and resentment create unforgiveness. We sometimes allow these feelings to remain, dismissing them as part of our humanity. Commit daily to examining your heart and inviting God's searching gaze into your inner being. As you do this, open yourself up to His scrutiny, allowing Him to reveal any hidden or anxious thoughts within you. Choose to be vulnerable before God, welcoming His correction, guidance, and transformation in your life. Seek His direction and leading, trusting Him to show you any path of pain you may be walking on and allow Him to guide you back to His glorious and everlasting ways.

REFLECTION

Consider any confrontations that you have experienced recently.

- How have you processed your feelings about what happened?
- Have you truly released the matter to the Lord, or is the sting of the moment still resonating in you?
- As a leader, reflect on the importance of examining your heart.
- Consider the significance of inviting God to search your innermost thoughts and reveal any areas that need His healing touch.
- Reflect on the vulnerability and trust required to open yourself up to God's correction, guidance, and transformation. How can you actively seek His direction and leading in your life, allowing Him to guide you back to His glorious and everlasting ways?
- Consider the importance of regularly examining your heart. How does it contribute to your spiritual growth?

AFFIRMATION

I am a leader who willingly examines my heart before God, inviting His searching gaze into my inner being. I open myself up to His correction, guidance, and transformation, trusting Him to reveal any areas that need healing or redirection. I embrace vulnerability and trust in His leading, allowing Him to guide me back to His glorious and everlasting ways. I release any remaining emotional hurt and anxiety to the Lord, knowing He will restore me.

PRAYER

Dear Lord, examine me through and through, revealing any hidden or anxious thoughts within me. I invite Your searching gaze into my heart to show me any unforgiveness or bitterness. Guide me on a path of self-discovery, correction, and transformation, leading me back to Your glorious and everlasting ways. Help me to be open to Your healing touch and redirection, trusting You to guide me in all aspects of my life. Amen.

NOTES

EXPERIENCING GOD'S PRESENCE

Do not yield to fear, for I am always near. Never turn your gaze from me, for I am your faithful God. I infuse you with my strength and help you in every situation. I will hold you firmly with my victorious right hand. Isaiah 41:10 (TPT)

MEMORY SCRIPTURE

DEVOTIONAL

Leadership is challenging and in certain situations, you can become fearful. Whether your fear is of losing your position, a crisis in the family, or a personal medical diagnosis that creates uncertainty about your future, God's presence is the answer. It is easy to feel overwhelmed by the challenges and uncertainties of life. However, we can find comfort and strength in the promise of God's presence. In today's passage, we are reminded that we do not need to fear because God is with us. This means that He promises to strengthen and uphold you in every situation. Embrace the opportunity to examine the profound impact of God's presence in your leadership journey, leading you to a deeper intimacy with Him.

PERSONAL APPLICATION

Commit to examining and cherishing God's continual revelation of the resurrection of Jesus Christ and His power and presence in your life as a Christian.

Seek to dwell in His presence and experience the joy that comes from being face-to-face with Him. Choose to prioritize moments of intimacy with God where you find peace, guidance, and renewal. Take a moment to reflect on a current challenge or fear you are facing. Remember that God is with you, and He is greater than any obstacle. Trust in His strength and guidance as you navigate through this season in your life. Allow His presence to empower and transform your life.

 REFLECTION

God's presence brings His peace that sustains us during challenging times.
Consider the joy and fulfillment that comes from experiencing His continual revelation of resurrection life.

- ✔ Reflect on the significance of seeking and cherishing His presence. How are you experiencing God's presence?
- ✔ Are there circumstances affecting your ability to recognize God's presence?
- ✔ In what ways can you cultivate a deeper awareness of God's presence in your daily life?
- ✔ Consider the times when you have felt His presence. How has it impacted your life during times of uncertainty? Allow these memories to remind you of His faithfulness and love for you.
- ✔ Reflect on how His presence has brought you peace, comfort, strength, and guidance. How can you practice moments of intimacy with God in your daily journey?

AFFIRMATION

I am a Christian believer who values and cherishes God's continual revelation of resurrection life in my life. I seek and dwell in His presence, experiencing the joy and fulfillment of being face-to face with Him. He is with me! Repeat this affirmation throughout your day, "I do not need to fear, for God is with me. He will strengthen and uphold me in every situation. I trust in His unfailing love and guidance."

PRAYER

Heavenly Father, thank you for the assurance that you are always with me. Help me to trust in your presence and find strength in your promises. May your peace and guidance be my constant companions as I navigate through life's challenges. Help me to seek Your presence and find joy, fulfillment, and guidance in Your nearness. Lead me on the path of life that You have for me and show me the eternal pleasures found at Your right hand. May Your presence overflow in my life, bringing joy and sustaining me through difficult times. Amen.

YEARNING FOR GOD'S PRESENCE

> *I long to drink of you, O God, to drink deeply from the streams of pleasure flowing from your presence. My longings overwhelm me for more of you! My soul thirsts, pants, and longs for the living God. I want to come and see the face of God. Psalm 42:1-2 (TPT)*

MEMORY SCRIPTURE

 DEVOTIONAL

Yearning is connected to longing or desire. We desire many things in life-success, recognition, healthy and happy families, and financial stability, to name a few. These things are important, but we cannot overlook the need to desire God's presence. As a believer, cultivating a deep yearning for God's presence is essential for spiritual growth and guidance. In Psalm 42:1-2, the psalmist expresses a longing to drink deeply from the streams of pleasure that flow from God's presence. This verse captures the intense desire for more of God and the satisfaction that comes from being in His presence. Embrace the invitation to cultivate a hunger and thirst for God's presence, allowing His streams of pleasure to quench your soul and lead you into deeper intimacy with Him.

 PERSONAL APPLICATION

Today, commit to cultivating a deep yearning for God's presence.

Seek to drink deeply from the streams of pleasure that flow from His presence, allowing His love and guidance to satisfy the longings of your soul. Choose to prioritize moments of intimacy with God, where you can experience the joy and fulfillment that come from being near Him. Allow your yearning for God to overwhelm you, drawing you closer to Him in deeper intimacy and relationship.

 REFLECTION

Reflect on what it means to you to yearn for God's presence as it is expressed in Psalm 42:1-2.

- ✔ Consider the profound desire to drink deeply from the streams of pleasure that flow from God's presence. What circumstances might be impeding your desire for God's presence?

- ✔ Reflect on the satisfaction and fulfillment that come from being there. How can you cultivate a hunger and thirst for God's presence, allowing His love and guidance to satisfy the longings of your soul?

AFFIRMATION

I am a Christian believer committed to cultivating a deep yearning for God's presence. I seek to drink deeply from the streams of pleasure that flow from His presence, finding joy and fulfillment in His love and guidance. My longing for God overwhelms me, drawing me into deeper intimacy and relationship with Him. In His presence, I find satisfaction for the longings of my soul and strength for my faith journey.

PRAYER

Dear God, I long to drink deeply from the streams of pleasure that flow from Your presence. Help me cultivate a deep yearning for You, seeking joy, fulfillment, and guidance in Your love. Draw me closer to You in deeper intimacy and relationship, satisfying the longings of my soul and strengthening me for my journey of faith. May my yearning for Your presence overwhelm me, leading me into deeper intimacy with You. Amen.

 NOTES

____

____

____

YIELDED HEART

MEMORY SCRIPTURE

DEVOTIONAL

Yielding your heart to God is the key to experiencing His will and transformation in your life. Recognizing areas of your life that are not surrendered to God is necessary to your growth and development as a believer. The word of God provides instruction on how we are to live well-pleasing lives that honor God. This requires us to be willing to sacrifice ideologies and opinions that conflict with God's word. In Romans 12:1, we are called to surrender ourselves to God as living sacrifices, embracing holiness, and delighting His heart through our genuine expression of worship. This surrender leads to a transformation of our minds that allows us to discern and align with God's good, pleasing, and perfect will. Embrace the invitation to yield your heart to God, allowing Him to renew and guide you as you lead with purpose and vision.

PERSONAL APPLICATION

A yielded heart is not a singular event. Rather, we must purpose to yield our hearts daily.

Often, the things God asks us to yield to Him seem almost impossible to surrender. In spite of the difficulty, we must commit to a yielding heart that is surrendered to God. Surrender yourself to God as His sacred, living sacrifice, embracing holiness, and delighting His heart through your genuine expression of worship. Choose to embrace

God's will and allow Him to transform your mind, renewing your thoughts and guiding you in discerning His good, pleasing, and perfect will. Yield your heart to God, seeking His direction and wisdom in all aspects of your life and leadership.

REFLECTION

Reflect on the transformation that comes from yielding your heart to God, allowing Him to renew your mind and guide you in discerning His will.

- ✔ Reflect on the call to yield a heart surrendered to God in Romans 12:1-2. Where do you recognize resistance within yourself?

- ✔ Consider what it means to be a living sacrifice, embracing holiness and delighting God's heart through genuine worship.

- ✔ How can you actively surrender yourself to God, seeking His direction and transformation in all that you do?

- ✔ What are some areas of your life where you are struggling to completely surrender to God?

AFFIRMATION

I am a leader. I will yield a heart surrendered to God. I offer myself as His holy, living sacrifice, embracing holiness, and delighting His heart through worship. I embrace God's will and allow Him to transform my mind, renewing my thoughts and guiding me in discerning His good, pleasing, and perfect will. My heart is yielded to God, seeking His direction and wisdom in all aspects of my life and leadership.

PRAYER

Dear God, I surrender my heart to You. Help me to yield myself as Your holy, living sacrifice, embracing holiness, and delighting Your heart through genuine worship. Guide me in embracing Your will and allowing You to transform my mind, renewing my thoughts, and discerning Your good, pleasing, and perfect will. When I struggle to fully surrender my heart to You, help me. May my heart be yielded to You, seeking Your direction and wisdom in all aspects of my life and leadership. Amen.

YOUR PRIORITIES

> *So think about the good things that are there in heaven above. Do not think only about things that are on the earth. Colossians 3:2 (TPT)*

MEMORY SCRIPTURE

DEVOTIONAL

Your role as a leader is often demanding. Perhaps your responsibilities create a disruption in your sleep pattern or affect your appetite. Leaders often struggle to create a culture of peace and contentment that sustains them and their team during challenging times. Aligning your priorities with God's kingdom is crucial for navigating the challenges and opportunities in your leadership journey. In Colossians 3:2, we are reminded to constantly pursue the realm of God's kingdom and His righteousness above all else. When God's kingdom and righteousness are our top priorities, everything else falls into place. Embrace the call to seek God first in all that you do, trusting that He will provide abundantly for your needs and guide you in your leadership path.

PERSONAL APPLICATION

What are your leadership priorities today?

As you lead in the workplace, your church, community, or your family, commit to aligning your priorities with God's kingdom. Be intentional in your constant chase after the realm of God's kingdom and His righteousness, making them your top priority in all aspects of your life. Choose to seek God above all else, trusting that as you prioritize His kingdom, He will abundantly provide for all your needs. Strive to keep your focus on God's kingdom values and align your actions with His righteousness as you move forward in life.

 REFLECTION

Reflect on the importance of aligning your priorities with God's kingdom in your leadership role.

- ✔ What were Jesus' priorities?
- ✔ Consider the significance of constantly pursuing the realm of God's kingdom and His righteousness above all else.
- ✔ Reflect on how prioritizing God's kingdom values can impact your decisions, actions, and relationships.
- ✔ How can you keep your focus on God's priorities in your daily life, trusting Him to provide abundantly for your needs?

 AFFIRMATION

I am a leader who aligns my priorities with God's kingdom. I will constantly chase after the realm of His kingdom and His righteousness, making them my top priority. By seeking God above all else, I trust that He will abundantly provide for all my needs. My focus is on God's kingdom values, guiding my decisions and actions as a leader.

PRAYER

Dear God, help me to align my priorities with Your kingdom. Guide me daily in constantly pursuing the realm of Your kingdom and Your righteousness above all else. As I seek You first, I trust that You will abundantly provide for all my needs. Help me to keep my focus on Your kingdom values and to align my actions with Your righteousness. Amen.

NOTES

YOUR PURPOSED LIFE

> **"** *: It is God who has worked in us to make us what we are. He has given us a new life because we are united with Christ Jesus. He saved us so that now we can do good things in our lives. Those are good things that he has already prepared for us to do. Ephesians 2:10 (TPT)* **"**

MEMORY SCRIPTURE

 ## DEVOTIONAL

Regardless of your birth order in your family, God purposed your life. Not only are you not an accident, but your life also carries meaning. You are a masterpiece, created by God for a specific purpose and destiny. In Ephesians 2:10, we are reminded that we are God's poetry, created to fulfill the unique destiny He has planned for each of us. Before you were even born, God had already prepared good works for you to walk in and fulfill your purpose. Embrace the truth that you are intricately designed by God for a purposeful life and that your journey as a leader is part of His divine plan.

 ## PERSONAL APPLICATION

Purpose is discoverable. God wants you to know why He created you, placed you in your particular family, in the city you live in.

Nothing about you was left to chance or was accidental. Commit to living out your purposed life as designed by God. Embrace the truth that you are God's masterpiece, created for a specific destiny and good works prepared in advance for you. Choose to walk in the purpose that God has uniquely designed for you, trusting that He will guide and empower you to fulfill His plan. Each day seek to align your actions, decisions, and leadership with God's purpose for your life, knowing that you are joined to Jesus, the Anointed One.

REFLECTION

What lies are you believing about yourself?

- ✔ Reflect on the truth that you are God's masterpiece, created for a specific purpose and destiny.

- ✔ Consider the good works that God has prepared in advance for you to fulfill.

- ✔ Reflect on the importance of aligning your life and leadership with God's purpose for you. How can you live out your purposed life as a leader, trusting in God's guidance and empowerment to fulfill His plan for you?

- ✔ Identify two areas of distraction which prevent you from fully embracing God's purpose for your life, and then prayerfully submit these areas to God.

AFFIRMATION

I am a masterpiece, created by God for a purposed life. I am not an accident, nor was I born out of time. My life was purposed and designed by God, and I embrace the destiny and good works that He has prepared in advance for me. As a leader, I walk in the purpose that God has uniquely designed for me, trusting in His guidance and empowerment. I am joined to Jesus, the Anointed One, and I know that I am fulfilling God's plan for my life through my leadership journey.

PRAYER

Dear God, thank you for creating me as Your masterpiece and designing a purposed life for me. Help me to embrace the destiny and good works that You have prepared in advance for me. Guide and empower me to fulfill Your plan for my life, aligning my actions, decisions, and leadership with Your purpose. May I walk in the truth that I am joined to Jesus, the Anointed One, and live out Your purposed life for me. Amen.

YOUR IDENTITY

> *For the Holy Spirit makes God's fatherhood real to us as he whispers into our innermost being, 'You are God's beloved child!' And since we are his true children, we qualify to share all his treasures, for indeed, we are heirs of God himself. Romans 8:16-17 (TPT)*

MEMORY SCRIPTURE

 DEVOTIONAL

Leaders who struggle with feelings of illegitimacy often struggle with leading authentically. Everyone has a need to belong, to experience value and worth. With so many parents not living in the same home as their children, some children struggle with feelings of abandonment or fatherlessness, constantly wondering who they are. Your identity is rooted in being a beloved child of God. In Romans 8:16-17, we are reminded that the Holy Spirit affirms our identity as God's beloved children, qualifying us to share in His treasures and making us heirs of God Himself. This profound truth shapes how we view ourselves and our role as leaders. Embrace the reality that you are deeply loved and valued by God, and that as His child, you have an inheritance of His blessings and authority.

 PERSONAL APPLICATION

Today, commit to embracing your identity as a beloved child of God who is filled with purpose and destiny.

Allow the Holy Spirit to affirm within you that you are God's beloved child, qualified to share in His treasures and inherit His blessings. Choose to view yourself through the lens of being a cherished heir of God, recognizing the authority and blessings that come with your identity. Lead with confidence and assurance, knowing that your true identity is found not in your parents or career titles, but in being a beloved child of God.

 REFLECTION

Consider your self-perception. How do you see yourself?

- ✔ Reflect on the truth of your identity as a beloved child of God, as affirmed by the Holy Spirit.
- ✔ Consider what it means to share in God's treasures and be heirs of His blessings.
- ✔ Reflect on how your identity as God's child shapes your perspective on leadership and influences your interactions with others.
- ✔ How can you live out your identity as a beloved child of God in your leadership journey, embracing the authority and blessings that come with being His heir?

 AFFIRMATION

I am a beloved child of God, affirmed by the Holy Spirit. I share in His treasures and inherit His blessings as His true child. As a leader, I embrace my identity as God's cherished heir, leading with confidence and assurance. My true identity is not found in my parents or my career titles, but in being a beloved child of God. Because of this truth, I walk in the authority and blessings that come with this identity.

 PRAYER

Dear God, thank you for affirming my identity as Your beloved child through the Holy Spirit. Help me to embrace the truth that I am qualified to share in Your treasures and inherit Your blessings. Guide me in leading with confidence and assurance, knowing that my true identity is found in being Your cherished heir. May I live out my identity as Your beloved child, reflecting Your love and authority to those around me. Amen.

NOTES

ZEAL FOR GOD'S KINGDOM

Be enthusiastic to serve the Lord, keeping your passion toward him boiling hot! Radiate with the glow of the Holy Spirit and let him fill you with excitement as you serve him!
Romans 12:11 (TPT)

MEMORY SCRIPTURE

DEVOTIONAL

Having zeal is not an automatic trait. Challenging seasons can rob us of the passion of zeal. Under the weight of leadership responsibilities, we struggle from day to day. Cultivating zeal for God's kingdom is a powerful force that can ignite faith and empower others to believe. In our scripture for today, we are encouraged never to let ourselves lack zeal but to keep our spiritual fervor as we serve the Lord. This fervor and passion for God's kingdom are contagious and can lead to transformation in the lives of those around us. Leaders must be passionate and enthusiastic about advancing God's kingdom here on earth. Our zeal should fuel our actions, inspire others, and bring glory to God in all that we do.

PERSONAL APPLICATION

Today, commit to cultivating zeal for God's kingdom in your life and ministry.

Be fueled with enthusiasm for the Lord, sharing your knowledge of Jesus with accuracy and passion. Choose to inspire and empower others to believe by demonstrating a fervor for God's kingdom in all that you do and are. Be ignited each day as you consider the amazing ways God manifests His commitment to you. Seek to ignite faith and transformation through your zeal for God's kingdom, impacting those around you and advancing His purposes in the world.

🔍 REFLECTION

Take a moment to reflect on your journey as a Christian leader.

- ✔ Have there been times when your zeal wavered? What was the cause?
- ✔ How can you reignite that passion for serving God and advancing His kingdom?
- ✔ Today, examine your heart and ask yourself if you are truly zealous for God's kingdom. Are you wholeheartedly serving the Lord with passion and fervor?
- ✔ Commit to being intentional in your faith, seeking opportunities to spread His love and light wherever you go. Remember that your enthusiasm and dedication can have a powerful impact on those around you.

AFFIRMATION

I am a Christian leader filled with zeal for God's kingdom. I will allow my zeal for God's kingdom agenda to be renewed daily. I will not simply exist as a leader, but I will thrive. I will seek to advance God's kingdom through my life and leadership each day. My passion and fervor for serving the Lord will inspire others and bring glory to His name. I commit to wholeheartedly pursuing His will and spreading His love wherever I go.

🙏 PRAYER

Heavenly Father, ignite a fire within me that burns with zeal for Your kingdom. Help me to serve You with passion and fervor, never lacking in enthusiasm for Your work. May my life be a reflection of Your love and grace, inspiring others to draw closer to You. In Jesus' name, Amen.

📝 NOTES

ZEAL FOR GOD'S GLORY

> *Whatever you are doing, show that God is great.*
> *When you eat anything, or you drink anything,*
> *do it all in a way that praises God.*
> *1 Corinthians 10:31 (TPT)*

MEMORY SCRIPTURE

 DEVOTIONAL

Kingdoms in the earth rise and fall, but God's kingdom stands forever! As you serve God's purpose in your leadership, there will be times of great honor, promotion, and recognition. You may be financially increased so that you can drive a better car, live in a better neighborhood, or wear clothing by your favorite designer. Beyond having "things," cultivating zeal for God's glory in all areas of your life is a powerful way to honor and magnify His name. In 1 Corinthians 10:31, we are reminded to do everything to bring glory to God, whether in the simple acts of eating and drinking or in the tasks we undertake daily. This verse challenges us to align our actions, thoughts, and motivations with the purpose of glorifying God in all that we do. Embrace the call to live with zeal for God's glory, seeking to honor Him in every aspect of your life and leadership journey.

 PERSONAL APPLICATION

Commit to cultivating zeal for God's glory in ways that honor Him. Strive to bring honor and magnify God's name in all that you do, whether in the ordinary tasks of daily life or in the responsibilities of leadership. Choose to align your actions, thoughts, and motivations with the purpose of glorifying God, seeking to bring Him honor and praise through your words and deeds. Honoring the accumulation of possessions above God is unhealthy and self-defeating because it will leave you forever dissatisfied. Approach every aspect of your leadership journey with a zeal for God's glory, recognizing that He is the ultimate source of all your successes and achievements, and in Him, you will always find your longings satisfied.

🔍 REFLECTION

Reflect on the impact of aligning your actions with the purpose of glorifying God and seeking His honor in all that you do.

- ✔ Reflect on the significance of living with zeal for God's glory in your leadership role.

- ✔ Consider how you can bring honor and magnify God's name in every aspect of your life, whether in ordinary or extraordinary tasks.

- ✔ How can you demonstrate zeal for God's glory in your leadership journey, honoring Him through your words, deeds, and attitudes?

- ✔ Reflect on your daily activities. How can you intentionally live each moment for the glory of God?

- ✔ Consider times when you consciously glorified God in your actions. How did it impact your perspective and relationships?

💬 AFFIRMATION

I am committed to living with zeal for God's glory. I seek to bring honor and magnify God's name in all that I do, aligning my actions with the purpose of glorifying Him. My words, deeds, and attitudes are guided by the desire to honor God and bring Him praise. I approach every aspect of my life and leadership with a zeal for God's glory, recognizing Him as the ultimate source of success and achievement.

🙏 PRAYER

Dear God, help me to cultivate zeal for Your glory in all areas of my life and ministry. Guide me in bringing honor and magnifying Your name in every task I undertake, whether simple or significant. May my actions, thoughts, and motivations be aligned with the purpose of glorifying You, seeking to honor You through my words and deeds. Give me the strength and wisdom to live with zeal for Your glory, recognizing You as the ultimate source of all success and achievement. Amen.

ZEALOUS FOR GOOD WORKS

He sacrificed himself for us that he might purchase our freedom from every lawless deed and to purify for himself a people who are his very own, passionate to do what is beautiful in his eyes. Titus 2:14 (TPT)

MEMORY SCRIPTURE

 DEVOTIONAL

Jesus gave His life to free us. We are not among those who resist God's ways and His plans. Whatever our lives were previously, we have been transformed. Our former sinful habits and practices are replaced by submission to Him. Addictions and other vices are banished from our lives as we receive His life. We don't choose our own path, but we discover His plan and design for us. Being zealous for good works reflects the transformative power of Christ in our lives. In Titus 2:14, we are reminded that Jesus sacrificed Himself to set us free from sin and cleanse us completely, leading us to be passionate about doing what is beautiful in God's eyes. This verse highlights the connection between our salvation and our response of zeal for good works that bring glory to God. Embrace the call to be zealous for good works, allowing the love of Christ to motivate and empower you to make a positive impact through your actions.

 PERSONAL APPLICATION

You were created for impact.

Zeal produces inspiration and motivation to have an impact on the lives of those we influence. When you are zealous, you have the spiritual capacity to stay committed to your values and beliefs and to live your faith in Christ daily. Fully commit to being zealous for good works. Allow the sacrificial love of Christ to inspire and empower you to do what is beautiful in God's eyes. Choose to be passionate about serving others, making a positive impact, and bringing glory to God through your actions. Seek opportunities to demonstrate love, kindness, and compassion in all that you do, reflecting the transformative power of Christ in your life and leadership.

🔍 REFLECTION

Reflect on the significance of being zealous for good works as a leader.

- ✔ Consider moments when your good works made a positive impact.
- ✔ How can you continue to be zealous for good works?
- ✔ Consider how the sacrificial love of Christ motivates and empowers you to make a positive impact through your actions.
- ✔ Reflect on the beauty of serving others and bringing glory to God through your zeal for good works. How can you demonstrate passion and dedication in serving others and making a difference in your community?

AFFIRMATION

I am a leader who is zealous for good works. The sacrificial love of Christ inspires and empowers me to make a positive impact and bring glory to God through my actions. I am passionate about serving others, demonstrating love, kindness, and compassion in all that I do. My zeal for good works reflects the transformative power of Christ in my life and leadership.

🙏 PRAYER

Dear Lord, thank you for sacrificing Yourself to set me free and cleanse me entirely. Help me to be zealous for good works, inspired by Your love and motivated to make a positive impact. Guide me in serving others with love, kindness, and compassion, reflecting Your transformative power in my life. May my actions bring glory to You and reflect Your beauty to the world. Amen.

📝 NOTES

____

____

____

____

____

____

ADDITIONAL NOTES

📝 ADDITIONAL NOTES

CONCLUSION

As you conclude this 70-day devotional, take time to reflect on the lessons you have learned, the growth you have experienced, and the deepening of your relationship with God. I encourage you to continue applying these principles in your life and to share testimony and insights with those you influence. You were created for a life of purpose and impact. Regardless of your age or where you are on the "traditional" leadership spectrum, you must commit to journey beyond your current capacity. I encourage you to meditate on the passages below. To the seasoned leader, encourage and empower younger leaders, especially those for whom the call to lead can sometimes be overwhelming. Let this passage guide you in understanding your call to lead young leaders: *"As for the young men, tell them also to control themselves wisely in how they live. You yourself must always do good things too. In that way, you will show the young men how they should live. When you teach the believers, be honest and serious." **Titus 2:6-8 (Easy)***

To younger leaders, your call to influence and impact the lives of others is a high calling. God has chosen you to be an influencer in the lives of your family, friends, co-workers, etc. He is sending you into the world to represent him in everything that you do. You are not alone in your journey, for the Holy Spirit is with you. There are seasoned leaders whom you will encounter that will help you along the way. May these scriptures also encourage you:

> ***1 Timothy 4:12*** *- And don't be intimidated by those who are older than you; simply be the example they need to see by being faithful and true in all that you do. Speak the truth and live a life of purity and authentic love as you remain strong in your faith.*

> ***Ecclesiastes 11:9-10*** *- Young people, enjoy your life while you are young. Do the things that you think are good. Enjoy the things that you see. But remember that God will judge you for all the things that you do. Do not worry about things. Do not let your body cause you to have pain. You will not be young and strong very long. We all become old too quickly. (Easy)*

> ***Jeremiah 1:7-8*** *– The Lord said to me, 'Do not say, "I am only a child." You must go to everyone that I send you to. You must say whatever I tell you to say. Do not be afraid of them. Remember that I will be with you, I will keep you safe.' (Easy)*

A final note to young leaders: do not underestimate the impact you can have in your youth. Be an example to others in your words, actions, love, faith, and purity. Enjoy your youth but remember that God will judge your actions. Do not be afraid to step out in faith and fulfill the calling that God has placed in your life. Trust in the Lord's protection and guidance as you lead with wisdom and integrity. Let your life be a testimony to others, inspiring them to follow Christ. May you continue to grow in your leadership and influence, making a positive impact on those around you. Embrace the opportunities and challenges that come your way, knowing that God is with you every step of the journey. Be strong and courageous, for the Lord is your strength and your shield.

I began my leadership journey in the home of my parents, prior to my salvation. Every task I was given and the responsibilities that were assigned to me were precious moments that helped prepare me for the future. When I received Jesus as Savior, my leadership journey intensified as I learned to walk and live as a disciple of Christ. I began recognizing the leadership capacity that God had woven into the fabric of my being. Over the years, as I have journeyed with the Lord, he has allowed me to encounter individuals who could mentor and encourage me. Even today, at every new chapter of my leadership journey, God allows me to encounter someone, read a book, attend a conference, etc., that impacts my life in such a profound way that greater impact is released through me. In other words, my journey continues. Commit to continuous growth. Don't let mistakes define you. Rather, use those moments as opportunities for growth. A future of impact awaits you!

Let's go!